Grief Is Dark, But It Can Lighten III

When Tragic Life Events Appear Impassable and the Trauma Too Difficult

Jesse Montanya

Table of Contents

Introduction

Sunsets

Mesmerizing; Symbolic; Calming

My first book on grief just focused on the process someone may go through when dealing with the death of a loved one. Grief is a complex emotional response that can be extremely difficult to navigate through. A myriad of emotions, including sadness, bitterness, guilt, blame, and despair, adversely affect daily living. Anxiety, depression, or both, can change you mentally and physically, as well as emotionally.

Grief can affect both your identity and your perspective on life. You may encounter physical difficulties such as fatigue, sleep disruptions, and severe headaches. Mental difficulties may include an inability to concentrate and irrational thinking. Emotionally, you can find yourself wrestling with existential or philosophical questions at the same time that you are trying to support your friends, family members, and loved ones. Your relationships can take a beating as well because of your tendency to isolate yourself from people you know—including those who might help you.

In the first book, I allowed you to see what to expect and made suggestions on how to resolve grief. There was a focus on having to feel it in a personal way before you start to heal emotionally. You discovered there is no blueprint or timeline for grief. I was determined to give you the feeling that I was walking with you and offered my presence and support so that your emotions eventually became less controlling.

Many people associate grief only with death. But that's not always the case. I have experienced a great deal of grief in my life, personally and professionally, and it wasn't always because of the death of a loved one. With the second book in the series, I identified the grief that occurs with major life issues, including divorce and poverty. Many of the problems with these major life issues are the same, and many of the same treatment modalities will help, but there are differences.

Healing grief caused by major life issues is difficult. There needs to be significant emotional awareness and self-discovery to determine what has brought about this adverse change in your life and your feelings. You are challenged to be engaged and committed to a therapeutic process that will create a positive transformation. You can learn life skills that will assist with healing grief.

This final book in the series covers another important aspect of grief.

Some grief experiences, often caused by a traumatic or tragic occurrence, are virtually impossible to recover from. Prolonged grief disorder (PGD) is a term used by therapists to explain the intense longing for a person who has died. PGD is diagnosed if the period of grief extends past six months. Grief caused by tragic life experiences and trauma severely changes you in ways that can become lifelong if you don't have an intervention such as treatment by a mental health professional.

It's important to note that grief is personal; it goes along its own timeline and is experienced from each person's frame of reference. How someone grieves is so individual.

You may have gained a certain relief from one or both of my other books in this series but still remain trapped with controlling negative emotions caused by the death of your loved one. I trust you will gain insight into the level of your grief through this book and will be able to live fully again despite your loss.

In this book, I cover certain severely tragic life experiences: the suicide of a loved one, death at the hands of someone else, not knowing what has happened to a kidnapped or MIA loved one, military deaths, early-life loss such as miscarriage or a SIDS death, and loss of a limb or a terminal diagnosis.

I understand that all deaths can be seen as tragic and traumatic. If you simply cannot determine how you can live your life after the passing of a loved one, if there has been time to process the emotions yet you still feel consumed by them, if your quality of life has significantly and adversely changed, then I believe there will be benefits for you when you read this third book.

Grief is complex and can be life-defining. It can be so consuming that it can feel like the end of life for those left behind as well. But your grief is unique and valid. I feel your pain. I know how it can change life so much that it can be difficult or impossible to see meaning for tomorrow. You suffer because of your intelligence as a human being. You suffer because your true purpose is to love and be loved. Yes, you suffer, but you need not suffer alone or forever.

When you at last heal from grief, you can also experience resilience and personal and emotional growth. When you integrate the loss and your feelings about it into your life, you can even experience a renewal of strength and purpose. Your life will be transformed.

I would like to direct your attention back to the previous books in my Grief Is Dark, But It Can Lighten series. In my first book, I asked your permission: "Allow me to walk with you." I never left your side. As we discovered grief in major life issues in the second book, I asked: "Allow me to guide you," and you did. Here, right now, my request is: "Allow me to show you peace." I will walk with you, guide you, and show you how there can be peace in your life after loss.

Your life may have been arduous up to now, but this is a pivotal time. I'll cover the tragic life issues that you may encounter and show you how you can live a fruitful life despite your loss. Allow me the time to relieve your grief and bring peace to your life so you can welcome tomorrow again.

***

As a professional counselor in Australia for over 20 years, I honed my abilities and skills by addressing my clients' difficulties. During the first decade, I primarily assisted individuals, families, and communities, particularly regarding a devastating drought that severely impacted essential farm workers and led to widespread stress and heartache. The ongoing turmoil caused by the drought presented significant challenges for those of us who were tasked with providing support for those affected during this difficult period.

It wasn't typical counseling where individuals presented assorted psychological issues for me to address. Instead, farm workers were in need of my services to help with their feelings of loss and desperation caused by the drought. Doctors often contacted me to visit someone in need, and I received numerous phone calls, mostly from distressed women seeking help for their husbands and partners. My appointments took place in shearing sheds, during fencing, in the truck on the way to watering points, or while checking on livestock. I would go wherever my clients felt most comfortable.

Australians are frequently seen as resilient and resourceful individuals, a stereotype often linked to farmers and pastoral communities. Many were hesitant to seek assistance. I needed to develop a style that could confront this long-standing perception.

"Toughen the fuck up" has been a common piece of advice for those confronting tough situations. Throughout history, Australians have experienced a degree of isolation, fostering a strong sense of independence. It was hard to work within ingrained belief systems that influenced people not to seek counseling. It just wasn't present in their understanding of dealing with problems.

Then, nature, in the form of the drought, caused them to reconsider.

My responsibilities encompassed conducting one-on-one sessions and leading counseling groups. Additionally, I participated in community development initiatives, conducted courses, seminars, and workshops, and served as a guest speaker advocating for mental health awareness and treatment of mental illness.

For the past 20 years, I have primarily worked in the remote regional and outback areas of Australia. I have relied on a statement to articulate my work: Professional counseling is a privilege when someone so desperately in need invites you into their life. They need you to address serious issues, simply because they cannot. There is no greater privilege!

Now, through my written word, I want to share my experiences and knowledge to help a greater population heal.

***

The beautiful peace flowers in my first book allowed you to reflect on universal symbols of peace. I invited you to pause with each chapter in my second book and experience the wisdom of words from inspiring people and leaders of our past. Now, just take a moment with each chapter to marvel at the beauty of nature. Breathe deeply and relish life experiences.

I have provided images of 12 of my greatest joys at the beginning of this introduction, each chapter, and the conclusion. This is meant to allow you a moment of reflection, to pause and momentarily break up your reading process. They are what drives me to wake up each morning and experience life in all its wondrous glory. Contemplate what your 12 greatest joys in life are. And after you reflect, choose to relish these in your life no matter where you are in your life's journey.

Section 1:

Types of Traumatic Loss

Chapter 1:

What Is Prolonged Grief?

Waterfalls

Hypnotic; Unrelenting; Re-energizing

Some people find that grief for the loss of a loved one extends for a great period of time. The symptoms do not decrease and are intense and persistent. It is important to understand that this is actually called prolonged grief disorder (PGD). Let's explore the symptoms, diagnosis, and treatment.

When Grief Doesn't Leave

Grief is indeed dark. For some people, that darkness lasts longer than for others. The first two books in this series dealt with the emotions, thoughts, and feelings that accompany grief. They explored how it can manifest and how the brain and mind react to it. In this book, I'll talk about what happens when grief lasts longer than normal and seriously affects your ability to live.

Some people believe that time is the only way to heal from grief. But really, it's not the only thing that can help. In fact, sometimes time doesn't help at all. Early intervention may indeed help you in dealing with traumatic grief, but that doesn't mean the process is going to be swift. When you grieve for a long time, you can expect that resolution will not be easy or something that can be accomplished in a few quick visits with a therapist. They can help, but you should expect treatment to take longer than that.

Grief can last so long that it becomes a psychological problem. You should not expect prolonged grief to be linear or proceed according to the order of the five stages of grieving that you've probably heard of—denial, anger, bargaining, depression, and acceptance. If that sequence is true for you, that's fine. But if you don't go through those stages in that order, don't worry. Your grief is personal to you. It doesn't happen the same way for everyone. Basically, your journey through grief is an attempt to regain meaning in your life after a death.

After that death, you experience not just the loss of a beloved person, but a loss of meaning in your life, a loss of normality, and a loss of what you thought you knew. You long for meaning and to be whole again. And you find it a painful struggle to reconnect with the life you lived before the death of your loved one. Your friends and family, normal activities, and the social world seem so far away that they're impossible to reach. Your grief remains unresolved. It remains a weight on your brain and your emotions.

Grief that affects your life in a severely negative manner is a recognized psychiatric disorder. PGD, also known as complicated grief, traumatic grief, or persistent complex grief disorder, can cause problems that interfere with your daily life. It's more persistent and longer lasting than normal grief, which decreases with the passage of time. If grief over the death of a loved one lasts longer than the acute phase of grief, which is a year or less (six months for children and adolescents), then grief is considered prolonged.

If it is accompanied by specific symptoms, PGD can be diagnosed by a professional. It's estimated that 7% to 10% of adults and 5% to 10% of youngsters suffer from PGD (Appelbaum & Yousif, 2022). Something mental health professionals consider is whether your bereavement has lasted longer than the cultural, religious, or social expectations of how you should respond to grief.

PGD was recently added to the *Diagnostic and Statistical Manual of Mental Disorders*, the premier reference book for psychologists and psychiatrists. This officially classifies it as a serious disorder that needs professional treatment. If your grief becomes a serious problem, you may feel unexpected emotions including bitterness, guilt, shame, anger, or a feeling that you wish you'd died instead of your loved one. You may not understand these feelings, but you may not be able to get them out of your head. You get stuck, and your grieving process is derailed. That keeps you from healing.

Why some people suffer from PGD while others don't is not really known. It may have something to do with your psychological makeup, your personality, your environment, your inherited characteristics, or a problem with the neurotransmitter chemicals in your brain.

Anyone who's been bereaved can develop PGD, but there are some people who are at greater risk than others. Older adults are more susceptible, and so are those who have suffered from post-traumatic stress disorder (PTSD), anxiety, depression, or bipolar disorder. Poor health, lack of social support, or family conflict are also associated with prolonged grief. Caregivers are also more prone to PGD, especially if they had been or still are caring for a partner or loved one. If your loss has been caused by tragic or sudden circumstances, PGD is even more likely.

If you have had at least three of the following symptoms nearly every day for the past month, you could be diagnosed with PGD:

- identity disruption (feeling like part of you has died)

- intense emotional pain, such as sorrow, anger, or bitterness

- problems reconnecting with your friends, doing things you previously enjoyed, or planning for your future

- emotional numbness

- extreme loneliness

- disbelief about the death

- avoidance of reminders of your loved one

- lack of belief that the death is real

- a feeling that life is meaningless

People with PGD also frequently experience sleep disturbances—in fact, 80% of them do (Appelbaum & Yousif, 2022).

Treatment

It may seem like the only solution to prolonged grief is to let it run its course. But that won't work. The very nature of PGD is that it doesn't lessen as time goes on. Fortunately, however, you can get better. The availability of treatment should give you hope. Even though you're suffering now, there are people who can help. You can find ways to lessen your grief and keep it from taking over your life. With the proper care, you can recover from PGD!

There are many places you can turn to. There are benefits to each of them, so you can choose the one that best suits your needs.

In Chapter 7, I'll talk more about your support system and how it can help you heal from PGD. For now, let's consider how you can begin to fight back against the disorder.

Medical Professionals

The place to begin is with your family doctor or primary care physician. You may be experiencing some of the physical symptoms that often accompany prolonged grief—poor sleep, diminished appetite, or fatigue, for example. The complications of this condition can include the worsening of conditions you may already have, such as heart trouble. When you visit your doctor, they may ask you to answer questions on a depression screener to reveal if you have complicated grief. While depression is not the same as PGD, it is one of the effects. The depression screener may reveal to your physician that there is something wrong with your mood. This will make it more likely that they will ask you questions that will indicate whether you have PGD.

Your general practitioner can also offer you validation and understanding. A good doctor will provide information and develop a treatment plan that will help you through the physical symptoms that accompany grief. They will be the most familiar with your baseline condition and can recognize how and when you deviate from it.

Of course, the best thing you can do is simply tell your doctor that you have been experiencing these symptoms ever since the death of your loved one. This will make them look more closely at the possibility that you are experiencing prolonged grief. It will help them rule out other conditions that mimic the symptoms of PGD, such as adjustment disorder, chronic illness or pain, or a hormonal imbalance. Knowing the difference can mean you receive prompt, appropriate relief from some of the symptoms that you're experiencing.

Your doctor will probably suggest that you take care of yourself physically. This is good advice. If you pay attention to your sleep habits, diet, and exercise, your body will be better equipped to deal with the physical and mental symptoms of grief. If you are suffering from the anxiety and depression that accompany grief, your doctor may prescribe you medication. Remember, however, that grief is not the same as depression, and medication often doesn't help. Another thing your doctor can do is refer you to a mental health professional.

Let's take a look at what a psychologist, psychiatrist, or other type of therapist can do for you.

Mental Health Professional

One of the possible feelings you can have while suffering from prolonged grief is not wanting to live without your loved one. If your PGD is causing you to think about suicide, don't just ignore it. You need help right away. Talking to a trusted friend may help, but the best idea is to contact a therapist or call or text a support line immediately. You can even go to the emergency room of your local hospital, where they will assess your condition and determine whether it is severe enough to require hospitalization. The emergency suicide hotline number in the US is 988. Chapter 10 of this book provides support information for other countries as well.

If you're not in an immediate crisis, you can look around for a therapist. Choosing a mental health professional can be a challenge. There are many kinds to choose from, including a psychiatrist, psychotherapist, or counselor. Many psychiatrists have waiting lists for their services, and insurance companies can be difficult about paying for therapy. Employee assistance programs often limit the professionals you can work with and may only provide for six weeks of therapy. Treating PGD will likely take longer than that. And rural areas may not have practitioners close to where you live. You may have a long drive to find one, but you should persist. Having psychological help is vital.

Look for a psychologist or therapist who specializes in grief therapy. If you can't find one, a professional who deals with mood disorders may be able to help. Look at their website to see what their specialties are. In addition to this, a website can tell you their credentials and may even have reviews, as well as directions to their office. Psychologists often work in organizations with more than one practitioner, so if one of them isn't available, they may be able to recommend someone else.

You can call and request an introductory appointment. Be sure to ask if they will take your insurance, Medicare, or Medicaid payments. You can also get a sense of how compatible you are with them, as compatibility can be an important concern.

You need to have someone you feel comfortable working with to achieve the best results. Your therapy will work best if your practitioner understands your culture and your history. They should have sensitivity concerning highly personal topics and emotions. You'll want someone nonjudgmental. You can determine whether you and the therapist are compatible in just a few sessions.

Remember that the decision is yours. You don't have to stick with a therapist who doesn't have the qualities you require. You can look for another one who is better able to meet your specific needs.

Here's a look at the kinds of therapy you may experience.

Cognitive Behavioral Therapy

Cognitive behavioral therapy (CBT) is an extremely important form of therapy that psychologists and other therapists often use in treating prolonged grief. It stresses identifying irrational or unhelpful thought patterns and replacing them with more realistic ones. In other words, it helps you develop better ways to cope with grief. It's effective in treating many different kinds of mental disorders including PGD and PTSD. One study found that CBT "resulted in significantly greater reductions in prolonged grief disorder symptoms" than regular types of supportive therapy (Boelen et al., 2021). It's recommended for children and adolescents as well.

CBT emphasizes countering thoughts that prolong feelings of guilt, anger, and shame and fostering emotional understanding and awareness. Another principle is eventually becoming your own therapist by doing homework, either in therapy sessions or at home. There are a number of techniques that can be part of CBT, such as narrative therapy, journaling, mindfulness, art therapy, bibliotherapy, role-play, and thought reframing.

You'll learn much more about CBT in Chapter 7.

Bereavement Support Groups

How can you combat the feelings of loneliness and isolation that accompany prolonged grief? Support from and social connections with other people is a very helpful strategy. Bereavement support groups are one means of getting this. These groups deal specifically with grief related to the loss of a loved one due to illness, crime, or miscarriage. There are also grief therapy groups that are more general and don't concentrate on any one particular form of loss.

The main benefit of these groups is that you are able to talk with other people who truly understand what you are feeling. Other people who have gone through the same tragic life experience can provide a great foundation for recovery to an improved way of living through those losses. The people in support groups may also share techniques that have helped them deal with loss. There is usually a facilitator such as a therapist, counselor, psychologist, or other trained professional to help guide the discussion.

You can find some bereavement support groups through hospitals, memory care units, nursing homes, skilled nursing facilities, and hospices, or your therapist can recommend one. You may also be able to find one in your area by searching on the internet.

Healing Rituals

Rituals are a great way to honor the deceased. They can encompass literal monuments and remembrances, such as dedicating a bench in a public park to your loved one's memory. They can also be symbolic occasions when you honor your loved one in a personal way—playing their favorite music or meditating on the anniversary of their death, for example. It should be something that is meaningful to you and that honors the memory of the person.

Rituals are most beneficial when you have already been through CBT or another form of therapy to guide you through the process of grieving, experiencing behavioral adjustment, and achieving emotional awareness. Until you have worked through your grief, healing rituals may only bring up difficult memories and out-of-control emotions that only prolong your suffering. Once you have made progress in processing your complicated grief, you can begin to think about what kind of memorial will be best.

Making Treatment Work

Just going to therapy isn't enough to heal your grief. If you show up at your appointments or support group meetings but don't engage with them and do the work that will change your life, you'll be wasting your time. You'll stay stuck in prolonged grief. However, there are specific strategies that will make your therapy productive.

The first step to take is to stick to the treatment plan that the mental health professional you've been working with has developed. A treatment plan includes which aspects of grief are causing difficulty to you personally. Remember that not everyone's grief journey is the same! It will also outline the process that the therapist will guide you through and the types of therapy that will be used. The treatment plan is reviewed by your therapist's supervisor if they are in a group practice. And it will be updated, usually every three to six months, to determine whether it is working as desired or whether your treatment needs to take a new direction or begin dealing with new issues that have come to light during your initial therapy.

Attending your therapy sessions is important, of course, but you also need to engage with your counselor and do any homework they suggest. This isn't just busy work. It helps you practice what you have learned in therapy and integrate new knowledge into your life.

Another good piece of advice is to take care of yourself. This means attending to your basic health needs such as getting proper sleep, eating a healthy diet, and doing exercise. If you do this, you will be increasing both your physical and mental resilience and your ability to navigate difficult times. You should also do your best to decrease the amount of stress in your life. Finding time to rest and relax will do a lot to alleviate the mental and physical symptoms you're experiencing. You may be tempted to withdraw from all your normal activities but keeping a daily schedule will help you maintain a sense of continued life.

Finally, reach out for help. Finding a mental health professional to work with is important, of course, and so is joining a bereavement support group. But there are other ways you can reach out as well. If you belong to a religion or a particular faith or spiritual tradition, you can gain support and comfort from the people who share it and from the rituals associated with it, especially those that address death. Your spiritual advisor or religious counselor is another resource you can tap when you need to talk about the difficulties you're experiencing.

You'll also want to recognize that there will be particularly difficult times, such as the anniversary of the death, the person's birthday, and any holidays throughout the year that your loved one isn't there to share with you. Plan for these occasions when they're nearing. It may be best not to be alone, for example. Let your therapist know when one of these difficult occasions is coming up, and they will help you prepare.

Key Takeaways

- Prolonged grief is different from "normal" grief. Normal grief usually lessens in time when the bereaved begins to cope with the death. Prolonged grief lasts longer and doesn't lessen with time. Time doesn't bring you relief from your suffering and your emotional reactions.

- PGD can cause you to be unable to continue with the functions of your daily life. There are physical and psychological symptoms that can plague and make you even more miserable than you already are. It can be disabling.

- If you're suffering from prolonged grief, you need some kind of help and a way to learn to deal with your emotions. You can start with your regular doctor and attend bereavement groups. Your quest for healing will most likely bring you to a mental health professional who knows about PGD and can use techniques, including CBT, to help you.

- In time, you will develop greater emotional awareness and be ready to honor your loved one and create rituals that will help you heal.

***

In the next four chapters, I'll begin talking about specific kinds of traumatic loss. You may want to turn to the chapter that addresses the kind you've suffered. It will help you understand what you're feeling and why your loss is affecting you the way it is.

Then, you may want to go on to Chapter 6, the beginning of the second section of the book, where I'll provide insight into preparing for recovery and guidance through actions, strategies, and therapies that address your symptoms and bring about relief from your symptoms.

In the third section, I'll take you through the rest of your journey through loss and provide resources that can help you. You'll learn how you can move through grief and embrace the new day and new life that you will come to know!

Chapter 2:

Suicide—What I Never Got to Say

Beaches

Rhythmic; Energizing; Unifying

The unrelenting pain of a loved one who has taken their own life can be immeasurable. Sudden death adds another layer of emotion when it is a suicide. Some of the grief emotions are amplified. The unanswered questions are torturous.

Your Emotions

It's hard to imagine the grief you'll feel if a loved one or family member dies by suicide until you experience it for yourself. It's also hard to imagine why a person chooses to take their own life. There are several reasons, but the most common one is depression. This is a very serious illness, and it can be fatal.

How can that be? Some people who suffer from depression feel so numb and despairing that they don't see any reason to live anymore. Other people with depression are in great psychic pain and just want it to stop. Or they could consider suicide to be the better of two options if they are facing financial hardship, scandal, or relentless bullying. They feel there is no hope of life getting better.

Surprisingly, even someone who's taking antidepressant medication can decide to die by suicide. That's because one of the effects of the meds is to give the person more energy. If this happens before the depression is resolved, your loved one or family member may suddenly have enough momentum to carry through their suicide plans.

No matter the cause, suicide is extremely painful for the people left behind. They are beset by disturbing questions that will never be answered. Why didn't I see the signs? Why did they do it? Why didn't they get help? Why didn't my love keep them from doing it?

There are also emotions that can be heart-wrenching and that leave the bereaved confused and distressed. They may have thoughts like *I never got to say I love you. I never got a chance to say goodbye. I could have helped if only you had reached out to me.*

Common reactions include the idea that the person who died by suicide was selfish, weak, or cowardly and that they didn't realize they had so much to live for. The truth is that your friend or loved one didn't realize how much their death would upset you and others. They only considered how much continuing to live would hurt them.

What does the bereaved feel? Shock and disbelief overwhelm them. In addition to the normal feelings of grief such as anger, disbelief, and sorrow, they may feel a sense of guilt. These emotions can be intense and profound, leading to battles among the various people who are experiencing their own reactions. If they're stuck in disbelief, for example, you may feel that they aren't grieving in the proper way. If they're irrational and wild in their emotions, you may believe that they are being overdramatic and making the trauma all about themselves.

Anger is another typical reaction. You can be angry at the person who died by suicide or at God or another higher power you believe in. You may also be angry with yourself or with others who knew the deceased.

The bargaining reaction is another one that you may experience. It's based on the desire to have your loved one back. Or you may wish that you had been taken instead of them. Whether you have a spiritual belief or not, there is an overwhelming desire to have the person returned to you—and *now*.

Of course, there is no timeline or exact pattern for grief. You experience it in your own way, in your own time, with your own flow of emotions. Your frame of reference will depend on your personality, your experiences, your previous experiences with loss and adversity, and even your culture and family. Your relationship with the deceased and whether you have a strong support system can also be factors.

It's almost impossible for someone else to comprehend how much you're hurting unless they have been through this kind of loss themselves. I know this because I have been touched by suicides in the past, both professionally and personally. I hope you will allow me to offer my support and guidance. I also want to reassure you that grief will lighten as you navigate through the trauma of suicide.

The Brain and Trauma

Trauma changes the brain, literally. Like PTSD, which PGD can be similar to, the trauma associated with a tragic death can be both psychological and physical. To understand this, you need to know more about how the brain reacts to trauma.

The brain contains millions of neurons and synapses that deliver messages between its different parts. The spinal cord also forwards those messages to the body, including the muscles and organs. Without your brain, your other bodily systems such as your heartbeat and respiration wouldn't work. This organ is also where emotions and thoughts live, along with memories, language, and decision-making abilities.

When trauma happens, your brain goes through certain changes that affect your functioning. Although we often think of trauma as being something like the experience of war, which can cause PTSD, the suicide of a loved one and the prolonged grief that accompanies it are traumatic as well.

Here's a look at how the brain reacts to trauma and what the effects are.

One of the main brain structures called the amygdala is in charge of your emotions. When trauma occurs, the amygdala gets bigger. This triggers the fight-or-flight response in your body. You could have less control of your emotions and a more extreme response to stress. As you probably know, stress can negatively affect your body, causing a rapid heartbeat and rapid breathing, among other changes.

Another brain structure is the hippocampus, which deals with short-term memories. When trauma enters your life, the hippocampus shrinks. You become less able to distinguish between short-term and long-term memories. You can have a hard time telling the difference between those from the past and those of the present. The initial traumatic event feels like it never stopped, leading to flashbacks. You may also experience short-term memory loss.

The prefrontal cortex also shrinks. It's involved with regulating thoughts and emotions. Prolonged trauma means that you can feel highly alert and scared. You could also be unable to express what you're thinking and feeling and get stuck in negative thought patterns. The fear, anxiety, and stress you feel can recur whenever anything reminds you of the original trauma.

Prolonged grief presents extra problems because the brain effects just keep going on even years after the original trauma has passed. The amygdala, hippocampus, and prefrontal cortex have been triggered and, as grief overwhelms you, they continue to have their negative effects. A chemical imbalance also occurs in the brain, involving cortisol, serotonin, and other neurotransmitter chemicals.

More research on the effects of prolonged grief on the brain needs to be conducted. Research on the neurotransmitters in the brain that affect emotional reactions will be particularly important. Different people experience grief differently, and no blanket statement can cover the process for everyone. Understanding the workings of the brain during prolonged grief will be easier to treat if we know more about the underlying mechanisms.

Understanding Blame

It may be difficult to understand the blame that can accompany grieving a death by suicide. It can take many forms.

You could blame yourself for not being able to prevent the death. That may also extend to other members of the deceased person's circle of friends and family members, which can cause your relationships with them to crumble. Maybe you blame God or another higher power for not preventing the suicide or the conditions that led up to it. Speaking of the conditions that play a part in someone taking their own life, you could also blame society for not offering the help your friend or family member needed.

There is still a lot of societal stigma around getting help for mental illness and a lack of social programs that deal with preventing suicide, especially among those who are both unhoused and mentally ill. And, of course, you might blame the person who died by suicide. You could feel angry at your friend or loved one, thinking they were weak or selfish.

There's a general lack of understanding of what drives a person to this act. The motivations are likely to be complex and not well understood. Often, as noted, there is depression at the core of them, but that's not usually the only reason. A businessperson or political figure could be involved in a financial or personal scandal and feel that suicide is the only way to avoid humiliation or legal repercussions. A child may have experienced bullying; if they see no way to stop it or feel there is nowhere to turn, they may become distraught enough to take their own life. It's not uncommon for students of middle-school age to die this way. Those circumstances can create a traumatic blend of grief, blame, and pity for those left behind.

Many years ago, I was being debriefed by a psychologist regarding sessions I was having with a client whose family member had died by suicide. One problem was the client's belief that they were responsible. The "blame game" was totally consuming my client. But this certainly was no game, despite the fact that it is a commonly used term that describes exactly what they were experiencing.

During the consult, the psychologist reminded me of the following: An individual who takes their life is often not in a state of rational thinking. They can be consumed by their irrational thoughts and belief system. Their behavior could be extremely erratic or, alternatively, the person could be the exact opposite—calm and collected, content in their resolve.

From their personal point of view and frame of reference, the individual who takes their own life believes they are rational in their thoughts and beliefs and their desire or intention to end their life. There lies the tragedy. A person who is acting with so much irrationality is convinced that they are coherent.

The referring psychologist advised me to work with my client's belief system by telling them: You have no control, and you're not able to control someone else's behavior. No matter what was or wasn't said, it would not have changed the fact that the decision had been made. The deceased was thinking irrationally and had no rationale regarding consequences. It was their decision. My client had no control over their behavior.

As I pondered and discussed this concept in depth, I incorporated the information into my counseling. Soon, my client was able to develop a different mindset. She was still well and truly grieving her loss, but the anger toward her loved one for committing suicide and the blame she'd claimed for herself ceased. She accepted that she was not responsible for or able to control another's behavior. Someone who was thinking very irrationally made a decision. Sadly, they believed they were acting rationally when they died by suicide.

The many questions my client had for trying to make sense of the tragedy subsided when she understood that she couldn't have controlled her loved one's behavior.

Crisis Support

What can you do if you're grieving the loss of a friend, family member, or loved one due to suicide? Be aware that there are many services and organizations that are there to help with your healing. I'll provide some resources in different countries for you to reach out to in Chapter 10, but here's a general overview of the types of help you can get.

Crisis support telephone, video, or text counseling can be an important consideration for emotional support. They can offer you guidance and reassurance. They are also a good information source for additional services. The individuals who work at crisis support counseling centers dedicate themselves to your safety and emotional well-being. Whether they are professionals or dedicated, well-trained volunteers, they can offer great assistance, not just initially, but throughout your difficult journey to recovery from prolonged grief.

You might not have thought of this, but you should contact your GP, family practice doctor, or primary care physician right away after the death of your friend or loved one. When you're going through the trauma of grief recovery, you can have physical symptoms as well as psychological ones. Your physician can help you with a treatment plan that keeps your body healthy. Your doctor can also refer you to a mental health professional or a bereavement support group affiliated with a local hospital.

Bereavement groups can specialize in different forms of death. A feeling of isolation can hamper emotional recovery, so a healing environment with individuals who have similar experiences can definitely aid recovery. Suicide survivor groups are one type of bereavement group, and they can help you as you try to process the death. They provide support as well as comfort to individuals impacted by this kind of loss. They can provide enormous comfort and support. There may even be members who have attempted suicide in the past who can provide a very personal testimony to what they were feeling and thinking.

Mental health professionals who are experienced with grief and the grieving process are invaluable. I'm a firm advocate of this kind of service and assistance. Inviting an experienced, trained professional to walk beside you during your emotional turmoil can greatly assist in your understanding of what's happening. A mental health plan can be tailored to your individual needs, changing aspects of treatment as you progress or experience setbacks throughout your grieving process.

The Focus Is You

Remember that other people's grief journeys will be different. The support of family and friends is crucial in these times, but the focus needs to be personal as well. What may help one person may not be as beneficial to someone else. The help you need may not even be a consideration for another person touched by the suicide. Accept this and realize your individuality. Heal yourself. Support and love the people around you but also practice self-love and do what is best for you and your recovery.

This book and the other two books in the series are a great way to gain insight into grief and the grieving process. There are many other enlightening books and different kinds of literature out there that will aid your understanding and your recovery from prolonged grief. Educating yourself will accelerate this.

Your grief journey is very personal. Even people who are grieving the same death will have different experiences and needs. And grief *is* a journey. Don't expect yourself to pass through it quickly. When you're suffering from PGD, knowing that the process is gradual will help you manage your expectations and keep you from giving in to feelings of frustration or impatience.

You're experiencing profound grief right now. It may seem dark, but it can and will lighten. I've seen grief lighten even in the most tragic of circumstances. You do experience much heartache and pain, but there is hope that you will get through it.

If your loss isn't covered by one of the next few chapters, you may want to skip ahead and read Chapter 6 and the rest of the book. Sections 2 and 3 will help you transition through the grief process and relieve your emotions. You are not alone!

Key Takeaways

- One of the most traumatic events in life is grieving the loss of a loved one who has died by suicide. Your emotions will be overwhelming.

- Your brain structure changes and creates chemical imbalances that affect the way you react to grief, both physically and mentally.

- Medical assistance is of utmost importance. A medical plan is beneficial not only initially but throughout the entire grieving process.

- Seek and rely on the different kinds of support that are available to you. These include your family doctor, mental health professionals, crisis support services, bereavement groups, and literature on the grieving process.

- Remember that you are not alone!

Chapter 3:

Death at Another's Hands

Wilderness

Peaceful; Calm; Serene

Trauma changes you! Without intervention, the impact of trauma can create cognitive impairment for life. Even with intervention, PTSD requires life changes for you to be able to function effectively. Like any scar, it is always there. You know it's there. But it's not terminal. Allow for peace in knowing that hope can come from hopelessness.

This book is not an instruction manual for recovering from trauma and grief. It's a guide to understanding your grief and taking the necessary steps to heal from it. I can't be with you every step of the way, but I can offer my experience as a counselor and a grief survivor to point you toward resources that can help, especially mental health professionals.

Traumatic Death

Coping with death changes a person. When life is taken away at the hands of another or you don't know whether your loved one is alive or dead, it can emotionally scar you for life. Murder is one of the worst things you can think of happening to someone you care for. Death in a war zone is another gut-wrenching tragedy for those left behind. And when a loved one is kidnapped or military personnel are missing in action, not knowing their ultimate fate is a situation that is almost certain to lead to prolonged grief.

When you hear accounts of these situations on TV or in other media, you shiver with horror and think how terrible it must be for friends, family members, and loved ones. When it happens to someone you love, however, you learn a new meaning of horror and terror.

The processes that accompany such tragedies are induce trauma as well. Dealing with the police or military officials, going through the justice system, and even being considered a suspect yourself, is trauma on top of the trauma you're already experiencing. Then, as time passes, if a killer or kidnapper isn't found or a missing person stays missing, you can experience a kind of fatigue, especially when people around you start avoiding you because they don't know what to say to you.

If a perpetrator is found, you may go through trauma at the hands of the judicial system's processes, reliving the death every time your loved one's name appears in the news or the killer or kidnapper appears in court. It's even worse if they agree to a plea deal or aren't convicted. Every time they come up for parole—or if they are paroled without your knowledge—you suffer the loss all over again. It would be surprising if you didn't develop PGD!

Grief in Disguise

When the death of a loved one comes at the hands of another, anger and hatred can damage you for life if you don't get help. Both emotional and cognitive interventions will be necessary for you not to be consumed. Getting back to a normal way of life seems impossible and, to tell the truth, it will be very difficult. It's not something you can get over with a few therapy sessions or a self-help book. It will take time and effort on your part.

You may not even realize you are suffering from grief for a while because you're so caught up in emotions such as anger, rage, and the desire for revenge. It's understandable because of the grave injustice and the actions that ended a life that you held so precious.

With military death, there can be the same emotions toward the military organization, your country for sending your loved one to war, and the people that they fought against. Revenge is not an emotion, but the desire for revenge is a psychological state that can continue to plague you and severely affect your thoughts and behavior.

You will still have all the emotions of grief that are associated with any death. The processing of your emotions will be similar. However, the difference is that some of them will continue to plague your way of life to some degree, depending on what interventions you have sought out. The grief remains. It may be hidden at times and outwardly expressed when you least expect it.

Also, you may experience a sense of disempowerment because you realize you were and still are not in control of what happened to your loved one. You may blame yourself for not being able to prevent the tragedy. You may think, *If only I had been there to protect my loved one* or *I wish it had happened to me instead.*

You torture yourself with questions like *Why did it have to happen?* and *How can I live through this pain?*

Your emotional turmoil can keep you from performing your everyday functions and leave you feeling helpless. Your relationships with other loved ones, friends, and family members will probably change as well, disrupting your sense of identity. Their emotional responses may be different than yours, as they will have their own thoughts and feelings about what happened. You can have misunderstandings with them or even distance yourself from the people you need most.

Because your loved one was touched by violence, you may feel fear as well. The sense of security that you previously had can disappear. The world becomes a more dangerous place to you. You may feel vulnerable for yourself and for the safety of your other loved ones as well. You may tend to isolate yourself and those you hold dear to try to protect them. Your isolation may increase because few people can truly understand your loss.

The death of your loved one also means the death of the hopes and dreams you had for them, for you, or for your family. A sense of disconnection or powerlessness and fear of the future can result. So can a feeling of abandonment. It's not logical, but it can be part of your emotional response as well.

All these varied, tumultuous emotions are simply the way complicated grief manifests in you. Feeling all of them may blind you to the fact that what you are really feeling is grief. You could get so stuck on rage and ideas of retribution that are focused outward that you don't look inside to see what your own needs are. And what you need is a path toward healing.

Emotional Aftermath

You may not realize it, but your brain and body have been suffering because of your grief as well. Trauma causes changes in the neural pathways and structures of the brain in ways that make you vulnerable to physical and psychological disorders in addition to PGD.

Anxiety disorders and depression can severely affect your relationships if you don't receive treatment for them. They lengthen your suffering and keep you from getting the help you need. In Section 2 of this book, I'll talk more about treatment from mental health professionals. After you finish this chapter, you may want to skip ahead to Chapters 6–7, where I provide more information. For now, I'll give you an overview.

Anxiety and depression are common when you've been through tragedy and traumatic grief. Anxiety can feel like you're constantly on edge, waiting for the next event that will crush you. It wears you out physically. Your brain releases neurotransmitters and causes the production of stress hormones that affect the body. Muscle tension, hand tremors, migraines, high blood pressure, rapid heartbeat, and other reactions are likely. If they continue, they can cause serious damage to the body, such as gastrointestinal or heart disease.

Depression also starts in the brain with neurotransmitters. A lack of the "feel good" brain chemicals like serotonin and dopamine plays havoc with your emotions. Depression isn't just feeling sad. It's a state of mind notable for its sudden onset and lasting debilitation. When you're depressed, you can experience numbness, a lack of interest in things that used to bring you joy, and an inability to cope with the normal functions of life. You retreat from society and isolate yourself. You can find yourself spending all day in bed or, paradoxically, being unable to sleep at night.

PTSD is possible in addition to PGD. Both PTSD and PGD are responses to traumatic events and may extend over a long time. They both can produce flashbacks, intrusive thoughts, nightmares, and difficulty functioning with the demands of daily life. Sometimes, complicated grief is misdiagnosed as PTSD, while other times they occur together, which makes treatment particularly important but difficult. If you directly see or discover the traumatic death, PTSD is quite likely in addition to prolonged grief.

You're likely to experience personality changes. You could have poor emotional stability and excessive moodiness at a subconscious level. Your loved ones may notice that your personality has changed. Or they may not, if they're too caught up in their own grief. They also may not realize how severely the loss of your loved one has affected you. If you're suppressing your feelings, you may present a calm surface to those around you while, inside, you're fighting with a tornado of confused, traumatic feelings.

Projection is a neurotic defense or coping mechanism that your brain uses to protect you from emotions that are too traumatic to bear. It's a form of emotional self-preservation. You displace the emotions you feel and project them onto the people around you. For example, you might take the rage you feel about the person who killed your loved one and direct it instead at the law enforcement personnel who are trying to catch them. A person demonstrating projection can become suspicious, untrusting, hypervigilant, and deeply skeptical about what they encounter in interpersonal communication and relationships.

Projection is called neurotic because there is a dramatic change in personality and behavior due to negative emotions. There is poor emotional stability and often excessive moodiness and sadness at a subconscious level. The term "neurotic" isn't used much anymore. Instead, mental health professionals speak directly about the various disorders and coping mechanisms such as anxiety disorders or projection.

Emotional projection and personality changes can continue into the future, becoming an integral part of your life. Other loved ones may just accept and endure the behavior changes, accepting that these are the ordinary consequences of a person having endured such heartache and trauma. They may not realize the depth of your hurt and the fact that you need both help and healing.

One helpful process for coping with emotional projection is self-reflection. Developing emotional awareness so that you understand your thoughts and feelings can help you identify and challenge your negative, unhelpful emotions and ineffective coping mechanisms.

The Help You Need

It's important for you to know that there is hope of healing from the trauma and grief. Trauma counseling can be very effective in promoting positive change if you are committed to the process. Belief that you can be helped and your grief lessened is necessary. You have to trust the process and your support team.

Your first step in getting help will probably be a discussion with your family physician. They can help you develop a comprehensive mental health treatment plan. They can also refer you to other treatment sources. They can evaluate your physical symptoms and screen you for disorders such as depression and anxiety. They may be able to prescribe antidepressants or antianxiety medications to take the edge off those symptoms.

Medication alone will not be enough to rid you of trauma and its aftereffects, however. For real relief, you need to see a mental health practitioner such as a psychiatrist, psychologist, psychotherapist, or other professional counselor. Ongoing psychological therapy is needed. This can involve techniques such as CBT, which encourages you to identify and counter the illogical thinking and unproductive coping mechanisms you have been trying in an effort to stave off your grief.

Be aware, though, that you may have some resistance to reaching out for and accepting help for your prolonged grief. You may feel that letting go of it is disloyal to your loved one. You may not realize how thoroughly that same grief has upended your life or that you do need help. You may be focused on fighting your internal battle and confused by your inner turmoil. Or you may be experiencing social isolation and not want to talk to anyone or even go to an appointment. You might even be in denial, believing that you don't have a problem that requires professional intervention or that help of that kind will assist you in recovering.

You can also turn to your loved ones for assistance in getting help for your PGD or PTSD. They can offer encouragement and bestow confidence in gentle ways to help you seek professional support. For example, they could take on the tasks of driving you to appointments with your counselor or picking up your medication. They can give you hope that there is the possibility of a positive change in the way you are living your life. When you have someone—or several someones—who support and commit to helping you, you can open yourself to the mental strength and unwavering love that will further your healing from grief.

Key Takeaways

- Traumatic life events such as the violent death or disappearance of a loved one can cause you to be controlled and consumed by negative emotions like hate and anger. You may also feel a desire for revenge.

- Without intervention, you can suffer personality changes caused by effects on your brain function that result from your deep trauma.

- You may find yourself projecting your emotions on people who aren't responsible for the death. These people may even be trying to help you. But your personality may be severely affected, and you can develop unhealthy coping mechanisms.

- Mental health practitioners are necessary to guide you through the process of recovering from the effects of prolonged grief. Your loved ones can be helpful and provide support, too.

- There is hope!

Chapter 4:

Early-Life Loss

Rainforests

Pure; Inspirational; Earth's lungs

When there is the loss of early life, it feels like a part of you has died as well. You question the meaning of life and everything associated with it—the universe, God, or a higher power. Nothing makes sense and nothing else matters other than the longing for the life you have lost. Your pain makes me want to call on all my knowledge and understanding to help you find peace.

A Life Not Lived

Life is not fair and never has been. You've often heard this said, blurted out by people facing what seems to them like an insurmountable problem or event in their life—perhaps a disappointment in love or the loss of a job. But their pain pales in significance when there's been an early life lost because of a miscarriage, stillbirth, or an infant or young child's death by disease or accident.

No one can truly comprehend it unless it has happened to them, too. Even then, your emotional reactions may be different from theirs. But the depth of your grief is unfathomable.

I can't take away the pain of such a loss, of course. I won't try to measure your pain or what your emotions should be. That's not what this book is for. What I will do is try to help you gain emotional awareness of what is happening in your life and help you as best I can to get through the complicated grief.

The trauma is profound when an early life is lost because of the sheer fact that you have been robbed of time with a precious being. You have created a life or been significantly important in this early life that has been lost. Now, you have not even been given the opportunity to experience the world with this young human to the fullest or even at all. It's extremely heart-wrenching not being able to experience life with your child and all that you visualized as you would journey through life with them. You experience extreme, confusing emotions. A great deal of time is needed before you can achieve rational comprehension and emotional stability.

Different circumstances of loss, such as whether a pregnancy was carried to term or how long the child lived, can affect the longevity and depth of your grief, the psychological and physical toll on you, and other life adjustments. But it's safe to say that your emotions will be raw and devastated for a time. It's hard not to hate the injustice of the loss or perhaps the higher power that allowed it to happen. Doctors and even you and your loved ones can also seem to share part of the blame for your anger and grief.

Grief has been known to make you question everything you believe in. Throughout the questioning, shock, and disbelief you feel, you may be tempted to say, "Fuck the world."

That's not too extreme a statement. Your raw emotions and your irrational behavior can be frightening for both you as you are going through this trauma and for someone witnessing their loved one in this emotional state.

Emotions of Grief

No matter what caused the death, your reactions to the tragedy will be extreme. Shock, horror, and disbelief are often the first ones you feel. You could feel numbed by the shock or tormented by the horror. Much of your cognitive processes will be confused and irrational, but they might feel right and appropriate to you. It's an extremely difficult emotional dynamic that's nearly impossible to control. The depths of your sorrow and grief are likely to overwhelm you, not just in the immediate aftermath but potentially for a long time to come.

Guilt and shame are common feelings when the trauma is caused by a miscarriage, stillbirth, or unexplained death such as sudden infant death syndrome (SIDS). A mother can be left wondering, *What is wrong with my body? What did I do to cause this death?* or *What could I have done to prevent it?*

You could also feel consuming, tormenting guilt or shame when the death is accidental—drowning, electrocution, a vehicle accident, or other sudden tragedy. *How could I allow this to happen? Did I do everything I should have to prevent it? Is it somehow my fault?*

In any circumstance, the guilt can eat away at your emotional balance. You may project blame onto yourself and onto anyone else who had a part in the tragedy.

In addition to guilt and shame, anxiety and fear can arise. You may well fear that similar tragedies will happen with any future pregnancies or other children you have. You may have anxiety that the same or another tragedy may strike your family. If your child died in a traffic accident, for example, you may have anxiety every time another of your children needs to cross the street.

Your anxiety and fear can be unconsciously communicated to the child, affecting their emotional development, too. A death from SIDS can easily cause fear that your next child will die from the same cause. The world can seem out of your control, which it is, but your anxiety and fear can make you try to control everything around you.

The isolation and loneliness you feel can be profound and further complicated by major depressive disorder. You may feel that no one else truly understands your loss or the depth of your grief. As time passes and your grief doesn't lessen, the people around you will go on with their normal lives while you feel you just can't. You could also feel a sense of envy about the people who have not suffered your kind of loss.

You know your life has changed forever. You can't see an end to your grieving or even a time when the pain will be less. Normal social interaction seems impossible, so you isolate yourself even from those who genuinely sympathize with you and want to offer you compassion.

Another natural reaction is an emotion of yearning and longing for the child whose life was cut short or never had a chance to begin. You may torment yourself with visions of the milestones in their life that you will never get to share, from birthdays and graduations to their marriage and your potential grandchildren. When other families experience these occasions, your longing may increase.

Of course, these emotions don't occur in isolation. You may experience a confusing combination of more than one of these reactions. You could feel both isolation and longing or anger and guilt. That's the complicated part of complicated grief. It can be difficult or impossible to say what you are feeling, making it harder to communicate with those around you. Also, since grief does not proceed in an orderly way along a predictable timeline, your emotions may change over time, with wild swings between them.

Contributing Factors

Depending on the circumstances of your loss, you may well have to deal with law enforcement officers, lawyers, EMTs, doctors, nurses, or other first responders. Many of these people will have been trained in dealing with families affected by trauma, but there are always a few who are insensitive and appear uncaring. In either case, simply dealing with officials can be exhausting and may increase a sense of numbness.

In cases of SIDS and some accidents, you may be questioned by police or medical personnel. Reliving the loss or being suspected of contributing to the death is a cause for wild swings of emotion including irrational guilt, anger, indignation, or fear.

As time progresses, you will likely have to deal with reminders of your loss such as when you get the death certificate, plan the funeral, and write an obituary. These events will have a tremendous impact on your grief, as you are confronted by your loss with every detail you are forced to deal with. Your emotional stability is bound to be tested. A funeral director who is used to dealing with bereaved people, even in tragic circumstances, can also provide support and understanding as well as guidance through the arrangements that you must make.

Your Support System

While you are in the first stages of dealing with loss and grief, it's important to have people around you who can support you. Loving family members and close friends are likely to gather around you and offer their support, even if they don't know what the best way to do that is. They can simply be with you, all day and night if necessary. The human connection is vital.

Your family physician or general practitioner is also a person you should turn to. They can monitor your physical health, which may decline if you forget to eat, drink to blot out the pain, or suffer bodily reactions to anxiety and depression. They can prescribe medication to get you past the initial trauma and will recognize when you are ready to stop taking it. A relationship with such a trusted medical professional is important. They should know you well and be able to tell how you are adjusting to your loss.

Your doctor can also point you toward other sources of support and understanding. This can include a referral to a mental health practitioner, bereavement support group, or a group that deals with the trauma caused by the type of loss you have suffered. Such groups will help you alleviate the isolation and loneliness you feel and give you a chance to grieve the young life that was lost. Bereavement support groups can often be found through hospitals and recommendations from mental health professionals. You can also search the internet for those that meet in your area.

The internet is a good place to find online bereavement support pages. Funeral homes may even have an online page where you can share information about your loss and receive messages, tributes, and condolences. Some also offer the opportunity to make donations to a designated organization in your child's memory or to plant a tree in their honor.

Mental health practitioners are a vital resource for you when you've suffered a tragic loss. There are professional counselors and therapists who specialize in PGD and other mood disorders. They offer you a safe place to open up and share the emotions you may have bottled up. They're trained in listening skills and trauma therapy. They know how to support you through your journey from grief to healing and can track your progress and guide you through any setbacks you may suffer.

Another way to make a human connection in times when your emotions become too much to handle is a local or toll-free 24/7 crisis hotline. They have experienced responders who can offer support in your time of need. These dedicated people have each caller's best interests as their priority as well as resources at their fingertips, so they can suggest what can benefit you best at the present moment.

There is also a lot of literature available on the grieving process, ranging from books like this series that cover the experience of trauma and grief to accounts written by people who have been where you are. You can draw comfort and hope from their experiences. They know firsthand the emotional trauma and grief you are going through. Through their narratives, you can get a sense of how someone else has dealt with the tragedy of the loss of a young life, how and where they found support, and where you can turn for understanding. They may inspire you and give you the comfort you're desperate for.

Ideally, you can use a combination of the various sources of help that are all around you.

Emotional Triggers

Once you have made significant progress on your journey toward healing, you may encounter setbacks. These are to be expected, and your counselor or therapist will know how to help you through them. You may think that you are adjusting but then be overwhelmed by the same emotions you felt when the tragedy first happened. How does this happen?

Similar to someone with PTSD, a person suffering with PGD can experience flashbacks and intrusive memories. They're very upsetting because they remind you of the original trauma. The things that stir up your painful memories are known as triggers. You may encounter a trigger suddenly and be thrown back into the immediacy of the tragedy as if you are experiencing it all over again. When this occurs, it can be extremely painful and even disabling. You may experience a meltdown no matter where you are, even if it's in public.

A trauma counselor can prepare you for encountering triggers and coping with your reactions to them. They will create a mental health plan that will teach you what your triggers are and when you might encounter them. This will be a plan developed personally for you because your grief journey is unique to you. Then, this knowledge base will help them develop an action plan with you to address your emotional, mental, and physical needs when triggers and extreme reactions happen.

Part of your mental health plan will be techniques such as CBT or a desensitization program that can help you "reboot" your brain and deal with your triggers and emotions. I'll talk more about this in Section 2 of this book.

What to Remember

Grief can lighten in time, but there can be aspects of the traumatic event that may require a life-altering adjustment. Early-life loss does stay with you, but it does not define you. Where you are in your grief journey will determine your exact needs, but your strategies should be guided by a mental health professional who can walk with you through the complexities of your emotions. Trauma-informed counseling will be necessary to help you deal with post-traumatic stress and emotional triggers. But remember that medical and mental assistance will address different aspects of your healing. They're both extremely important.

Trauma causes changes within the brain. Aspects of your personality, emotions, and belief systems can change. Trauma and grief can make you dissociate, leaving you with the feeling that your brain is not a part of you. The powerful supercomputer that is your brain simply refuses to respond to your commands. It needs resetting. This takes time and effort that you won't be able to find the strength for at first. But as grief begins to lessen, the out-of-body sensation will, too.

You may want to skip ahead to Section 2 of this book, which goes into more detail about emotional awareness and how mental health professionals can lead you to a greater level of healing from your prolonged grief. The information I share in those chapters is designed to help you along your journey through confusing emotions and intense sorrow to a new sense of peace. I'll show you how you can find relief from the turmoil you feel and adjust to the new life you will live after you process your loss.

Key Takeaways

- When you experience the loss of a life that is in its early stages, the trauma will be profound. You will feel that you've been robbed of the time that you would have been able to spend with your beloved child. You will suffer because now you can't experience the world in its fullness with this special human being.

- Your level of grief will change as time passes. It will eventually lessen, but there can be setbacks along the way. Contributing factors including the circumstances of your loss and the support system you have around you will make a difference. That support system can consist of family, friends, and loved ones, but it should also include your family doctor and professional mental health practitioners trained in trauma and grief issues. Bereavement groups and crisis lines can help, too, and so can reading about the process of grieving. However you access it, a human connection is very important for your recovery.

- Because you have suffered trauma, there can be triggers that will make you experience the tragedy all over again. It's similar to what happens in cases of PTSD. Your reaction to triggers can be very upsetting and frightening—flashbacks, nightmares, and intrusive thoughts are examples of what you may experience. A mental health professional can help you learn what your triggers are and how to avoid or lessen their power over you.

Chapter 5:

Transformative Grief

Baby Animals

Joyful; Playful; Companionship

When a loved one suffers a sudden and permanent incapacitation due to a medical occurrence or an accident, or when there is a diagnosis of a terminal illness, grief is profound and complex. You are faced with a life transformation. With such a prognosis, you experience defining moments of adjustment that require another level of emotional endurance. The grief you experience, the courage you require, and your acceptance of fate are an extreme test of human tolerance.

Overwhelming Emotions

Certain life events pitch you into a storm of emotions right away. One of these is suffering the loss of function or the complete loss of some or all of your limbs because of a spinal cord injury, stroke, or other traumatic incident. It can change your life forever, and your emotions will be complex, confused, and confusing.

At first, you will feel shock and disbelief. No one expects to have this suddenly happen to them. Your life changes in an instant when a car hits yours or an IED explodes near you. You struggle to understand why this happened to you, and there are no good answers. It's difficult to understand what you will have to endure because of it.

What you will be feeling is a form of grief. You will go through all the same emotions as someone who has lost a friend or loved one to suicide or murder. Although your grief will have its own course and its own timeline, you'll feel anger, depression, bargaining, and denial.

You can feel frustration at the new limitations you face and anger at the unfairness of the situation. You could also feel anxiety and fear because you're unsure about the future and how much you can expect to heal physically. You can also feel hope that your condition could be reversible and despair if you find that that isn't so. You can feel blows to your self-esteem and body image that you must adjust to. You may also feel isolation and loneliness as you try to adjust to limited mobility and other people's tendency to stare at or ignore you. Very likely, you will experience a mix or a succession of all these feelings.

You should be aware that being eternally positive is not something that's required of you. You don't owe it to the world to be a shining example of good feelings and accomplishment. The transformation in your life means hardships as well. Everyday tasks can be not just difficult but impossible for you. Expecting yourself to be unrelentingly inspirational is not realistic. You don't owe it to anyone to be a poster child for conquering disabilities.

Authentic emotions, whether others define them as positive or negative, are valid and not to be stifled. Your emotions may change as you go through your grief journey but trying to force them into a mold isn't realistic. You feel what you feel, and no one should tell you what those feelings should be.

Too often, the media portrays the physically challenged as unfailing sources of inspiration. You often hear stories of how a person with a physical or mental disability is taken to the prom by a classmate, for example. This is presented as some kind of sacrifice on the classmate's part or a great act of charity. Some people in the disability rights movement refer to this as "inspiration porn" and argue that it's actually demeaning rather than uplifting. Just as toxic is the emotion of pity. You are who you are, and you don't deserve to have your struggles held up for public display.

Receiving a diagnosis of a terminal illness such as ALS, organ failure, or certain types of cancer will also subject you to emotional upheaval. Some of the emotions will be comparable to what you experience with any kind of loss: denial, frustration, anguish, and grief. Others will be specific to the fact that you can't expect to survive.

You may feel fear of death and anxiety about metaphysical questions about what happens to you after death. You could feel dread if your condition will require painful, distressing treatments that are doomed to ultimate failure at some point in the future. You can feel desperation as you long for a cure that might be created in time for you to live. You may feel regret over any unfinished business there might be, such as unresolved family trauma or dreams you've had that may now never be fulfilled.

Remember that your brain undergoes changes when you experience trauma. It responds with neurotransmitter chemicals and structural changes that affect both your body and your mind. Depression and anxiety are two of the most destructive results. Your mind can also seem to shut down and leave you feeling emotionally numb. You may have difficulty making sense of what's happening around you. Your state of mind can limit your comprehension. The reactions of your friends and loved ones to your new situation can also influence how you feel. If they react with horror or despair, you're more likely to experience these feelings as well.

Transformation

Medical conditions like these can elicit other emotions as well—positive ones. If you've experienced the physical limitations of limb loss or loss of function, you can experience emotions that will transform you. Over time, you may find renewed strength in hope and resilience.

You could discover your own ability to respond to grief with the determination to reclaim as much of your life as possible. You could come to an acceptance of your limitations but find the courage to live as fully as possible despite them. You could feel gratitude for the fact that you're still alive and able to function in new ways that bring you happiness, such as wheelchair sports; you could be grateful for the love and support you receive from family, friends, physical therapists, and other medical personnel. You can feel pride in your ability to develop coping mechanisms to deal with any limitations as well as difficult emotions.

A terminal diagnosis can fill you with more than strictly negative emotions as well. You could look back on your life so far with reflection on what you've accomplished and gratitude for the opportunities you've had and the beloved people in your life. Pleasant nostalgia can occupy your mind. You may find peace and even hope in the religious or philosophical beliefs you hold. You may find yourself engaging in meaningful opportunities or doing the things you've always wanted to do. And the more you can keep control of your surroundings and participate in your medical treatment, the more energy and power you'll feel.

Transformative grief comes with a number of positives. You can grow emotionally, with grief leading to increased strength and resilience. You could also experience a search for meaning in the face of loss. For example, you might reassess your relationships with family members, loved ones, and friends.

Grief can lead to a change in your priorities, career choices, and even your lifestyle. It can make you question everything you thought you knew and ponder what your values are and what's important to you. Or grief can become a spiritual journey. Exploring existential questions or the teachings of religion or spirituality can add peace and comfort to your experience of the struggles you face.

You may also find yourself forging new relationships with people who are in the same situation you are in. They can give you much-needed perspective as well as the wisdom of their experience. You may add them to your list of close friends. You'll likely find that the relationship is reciprocal. You will have wisdom and encouragement to share with someone else, too.

Transformative grief means integrating your struggles into your life story. Rather than trying to get over the grief, you incorporate the things you've learned about yourself and the world around you into your mental and emotional processing. In a sense, you redefine your life, and you can change the meaning of your story.

These positive feelings hold the power of transformation. They can bring you up from the depths of despair to a place of peace and even joy. You can transform your feelings and reality into something positive. You can get involved with organizations and charities that raise money and promote empowerment for the people who share your condition. You can thereby spread your renewed commitment to life to countless other people.

Your renewed spirit will allow you to share your positive attitude with friends, family, and loved ones. They'll share their love with you in return. Instead of feeling isolated and lonely, you'll have people around you who *want* to be around you. If you reach this level of acceptance, it can make life less distressing for everyone.

Medical and Hospice Resources

In developed countries, we're fortunate to have many resources available to help with the everyday struggles of people with limb amputations or paralysis and those with terminal diagnoses. They're integral parts of your support team. If family caregivers are bearing too great a burden, remember that there are people whose job it is to help. Some things are simply beyond what a family member can do.

No matter how strong you are, make use of these resources any time you need help. Their special professional skills and empathetic abilities are crucial to your well-being and dignity. They're dedicated members of the helping professions and available to help you, whatever your physical and emotional needs.

Here are some of the multidisciplinary professionals who can make your life easier.

Medical Resources

For the traumatic loss of limb function, you will likely have emergency room personnel and an orthopedic surgeon who will help with the initial trauma, advise you on the extent of your injuries, and tell you what can be done surgically. If paralysis is your problem, a neurologist will likely oversee your care.

A physical medicine and rehabilitation specialist, also called a physiatrist, will be part of your team. Their role is to restore as much function in your limbs as possible and help you improve your quality of life.

Prosthetists can be called on to recommend and fit an artificial limb if you've lost one or more of yours. Great advances have been made in recent years. Depending on your insurance coverage and monetary resources, prosthetic devices can vary from artificial limbs to devices that rely on electrical impulses or ultra-modern "Blade Runner" technology.

Both a physical therapist and an occupational therapist will be part of your team of professionals. Your physical therapist will help you regain as much function as possible, as well as strength and independence. They can also develop a personalized exercise routine for you. An occupational therapist will help you learn to perform daily living tasks in order to achieve greater independence after limb-function loss.

An orthopedic physiotherapist specializes in the musculoskeletal system. They can help with targeted exercise programs to improve your range of motion and address specific issues with your rehabilitation.

Rehabilitation nurses also have an important part to play in your healing. They provide education and help co-ordinate your care. They play an integral part in helping you adjust to your challenges and manage your healthcare.

There are psychologists or counselors who specialize in rehabilitation and trauma. They can help you cope with the emotional fallout of your injury. When you need to develop strategies for adjusting to your new reality, they are a resource you can turn to for support.

You may not realize it, but social workers are an important part of your care team as well. They can help you navigate the complexities that inevitably arise when you're dealing with insurance companies. They can help you find a rehab facility that takes your insurance when you are ready to leave the hospital, for example. They also help families and put you in touch with local groups that can assist you.

Case managers co-ordinate your healthcare and know when to bring in additional specialists you may need. Their specialty is co-ordination and planning. They help you and your caregivers navigate through the many people and resources available to you.

You can also get a lot of help from a peer mentor who, like you, has suffered limb loss or loss of function. They can help you develop a sense of community to let you know that you're not alone. Through their experience with a challenge like yours, they also promote understanding and put you in touch with the resources and organizations that have helped them.

A vocational rehabilitation specialist helps with getting you ready to re-enter the workforce or develop new vocational goals. Counseling, job training, and support are their specialties.

Hospice Resources

If you've been diagnosed with a terminal illness, you may find yourself going into a hospice facility. It's not just a place to go to die, as many people think. In reality, these are places where a team of professionals assist you in maintaining your quality of life and relieving your suffering. Hospice services can be provided at home or in a specialized facility. They field a team of professionals who specialize in three things: emotional support, pain management, and symptom relief. Here are the personnel you may need.

The medical director of the hospice is a doctor who oversees your medical care. They co-ordinate with your physicians to create and adjust a care plan for you. They work in concert with your primary physician and other members of your care team.

Hospice nurses can be either registered nurses or licensed practical nurses. They're the people responsible for providing direct care to you, whether you're in your home or a hospice facility. They administer medications, assess symptoms, and give advice on managing them. They also provide valuable emotional support for both you and your family.

Nurse practitioners have received more training than registered nurses or licensed practical nurses. They work with the medical director and can prescribe medications. Nurse practitioners also assist families by providing emotional support and education.

There are hospice social workers, too, much like hospital social workers. They help you and your family navigate the complexities of the financial, insurance, and advanced-care planning needs. They also know about community resources and can put you in contact with them.

You and your family can get emotional or spiritual help from the hospice chaplain or spiritual-care provider. Among their primary duties are providing comfort and helping families with discussions about life, death, and what happens afterward. They care for anyone, regardless of religious or spiritual beliefs.

Hospice aides are certified nursing assistants who are involved in your day-to-day care. They help ensure comfort and dignity by providing care such as bathing, grooming, and mobility. They'll be the people whom you see every day for most of your physical needs other than medical concerns.

Hospice volunteers are vital members of the hospice community. In addition to providing emotional support, they spend time with patients, provide respite for family members, and guide activities for patients. They take some of the burdens off of caregivers of all types and establish personal relationships with you and your family.

A bereavement coordinator or counselor provides support to family members both before and after the loss of their loved one. They can put families in touch with bereavement or grief support groups and offer emotional support.

As they do at hospitals, physical and occupational therapists can help with managing pain, helping with mobility issues, and working for your comfort and independence. Speech-language pathologists can also help with communication and potential swallowing difficulties.

The hospice pharmacist works with the doctors and nurse practitioners to deliver the optimum level of symptom control and pain management.

A hospice may also employ art and music therapists to assist with emotional well-being and creative outlets that can help you express yourself and provide additional ways to communicate your feelings.

Having all these professionals to care for you helps ensure that all your needs are met. They can develop a personalized care plan to cover all aspects of your comfort and well-being. They will help preserve your dignity and meet your personal needs as you approach the end of your life.

Family and Friends

Significant physical challenges and serious medical conditions place burdens on family, friends, and loved ones as well. Their natural concern for you can be uplifting, but it can also feel like a burden to you. They'll go through some of the same emotional changes that you do. They'll also have concerns of their own. As much as you want them not to be caught up in grief and other negative emotions, there's no real way to prevent it. You can try to keep up a positive attitude, but if you're not at the point where you genuinely feel that kind of transformation, your loved ones will likely sense that you're in emotional pain—putting on a brave face when you don't feel it may not reassure them.

Your family members and friends may also try to stay positive despite emotional turmoil. This is good if it's genuine, but if they're not feeling it inside, they can easily break down under the stress. It's a delicate balance between sharing your true feelings and covering up any negative thoughts and feelings. It's just not realistic for either you or them to be happy all the time. Your condition is naturally a cause for concern.

Your family and loved ones may take on some of the tasks of caregiving that hospital nursing personnel or private duty staff aren't able to provide. The mental and emotional stress of caregiving will take a toll. They're likely to need a break at times. If they can call on other people to take over for them, it will help them be able to provide optimal care. They will also need to hear positive reinforcement that they're doing a good job of caring for you. If you can offer it to them, it will definitely be appreciated.

Caregiver respite services provide much-needed opportunities for family caregivers to step out of their vital but often-draining roles for a while. This gives them a chance to restore their stamina and energy. Fortunately, most areas provide these resources for caregivers to enable them to carry on doing the best for their loved ones. Here are some places that can offer respite care.

The ARCH National Respite Network and Resource Center has a website where their National Respite Locator Service can put you in touch with respite caregivers in your area. State Aging and Disability Resource Centers, also known as ADRCs, can also assist you. The contact information for your state's ADRC will be on the Eldercare Locator website.

Many locations around the country have an Area Agency on Aging. Search online to find yours. They can offer a variety of information and assistance.

If your needs are service-related, the Veterans Administration (VA) offers respite care services for family caregivers. Either your local VA office or the VA's website can give you more information on what's available and how to access it.

The American Association of Retired Persons and disease-specific organizations such as the Alzheimer's Association may be able to put you in touch with local sources of respite care services. Local chapters of these organizations may also be able to put you in touch with places where respite services are available.

You may also be able to find help from local and faith-based organizations. Churches and synagogues, as well as community organizations, sometimes offer respite services as part of their mission to improve people's lives.

Setbacks

You will experience setbacks with the trauma and hardship you have encountered. There can be relapses of your condition, complications from medical treatment, or just being down in the emotional dumps when your positive attitude falters. But you have resources that can help you with these roadblocks and disappointments.

The most important of your helpers will be the medical personnel who monitor your condition and provide aid. They can offer you advice, alternatives, and general support when you need it.

If you have a mental health professional on your support team, you can turn to them when you are overwhelmed with negative emotions such as denial or despair. You can tell them anything, even things you can't tell anyone else. Everything you tell them will be held in strictest confidence. They will share techniques with you that can help you deal with emotional trauma and give you a safe place to reveal your authentic emotions.

The grief that accompanies impending death or chronic incapacitation can feel overwhelming. Take advantage of every opportunity and resource you have to make the transition easier. If you can summon courage and a way to combat the emotional instability that you face, you can better negotiate the course of your life. These traits are not learned and may not be immediately forthcoming.

There will be victories, and there will be dark moments, but, hopefully, there will also be moments that engage the essence of life.

Inspiration and Love

I am inspired by role models. I marvel at physically challenged athletes and other famous people—how they are driven, and their massive positive impact on society. Don't you think many of them also had dark moments through their recovery? Even with fame and being in the celebrity spotlight, they have also faced mental and emotional challenges at times.

It's easy to be inspired by their resilience and the perseverance that was required for them to rise to lofty heights considering the challenges they faced. I have followed the careers of special individuals and been uplifted, not just by their astounding performances in their careers, but by their personalities and stories. Their accomplishments exemplify the caliber of these extraordinary human beings. Their disabilities fade from view.

Here are some champions whose stories can inspire you, too.

Christopher Reeve

Handsome and talented, U.S. actor Christopher Reeve was best known for playing Superman and other roles in movies. His life changed in a moment when he was just 42, with his career still ahead of him. Then, his horse fell during an equestrian competition. Reeve landed on his head and a spinal cord injury instantly rendered him paralyzed from the shoulders down. He lost the ability to breathe on his own, so he had to use a ventilator.

For the remainder of his life, Reeve voiced his determination to someday walk again. His doctors didn't approve of him speaking about this, as very few people with severe spinal cord injuries recover enough to walk on their own. While he never became able to walk again, Reeve did make significant progress; he could move his fingers and toes and experience stimuli such as heat and coldness on his skin.

Reeve also became a noted activist, promoting research for spinal cord injuries and controversial therapies such as stem cell research. He established a foundation that he hoped would enable people with paralysis and other conditions such as Parkinson's disease. He also opened a paralysis resource center to promote more independent living for people with similar conditions.

Madison de Rozario

Australian Paralympic athlete and wheelchair racer Madison de Rozario developed transverse myelitis, a form of spinal cord injury, when she was four, causing her to lose the use of her legs. She was encouraged to begin wheelchair racing by Frank Ponta, himself an inductee into the Australian Paralympic Hall of Fame. When she began her racing career at age 14, Madison was the youngest member of the Australian Paralympic Team.

De Rozario's career has been stellar. She has traveled all over the world competing in professional middle- and long-distance events. She has at least 20 different medals and holds two world records. She has also won the Oz Day 10K Wheelchair Road Race nine times between 2012 and 2023. She promotes Paralympic events on social media.

Wilma Rudolph

Wilma Rudolph's sports career had an unlikely beginning. In childhood, she suffered from both polio and scarlet fever. She wore a brace on her leg and was told she would never walk again. Her parents and the 21 other children in the family took care of her; they massaged her leg while she took off her brace. By the age of six, she had begun to hop on one leg, and by age 11, she was outside playing basketball. She continued playing in high school, but a coach recommended that she try track and field events. Even though she was still in high school, Rudolph competed at the collegiate level.

Rudolph represented the US in the 1956 Melbourne Olympic Games, which was her first time out. She won a bronze medal in a relay event. At the next Olympics, she won three gold medals and broke three world records. After that, she was hailed as the fastest woman in the world.

After her track and field career, she returned to college to study for her degree and worked in the educational field. She took a stand for civil rights when she refused to attend a homecoming parade because it was segregated. She also started a foundation to help amateur track and field athletes.

Dylan Alcott

Just a few weeks after he was born, Dylan Alcott needed surgery for a tumor wrapped around his spinal cord. The operation removed the tumor, but Alcott was left a paraplegic. He had a difficult time dealing with his condition, but an interest in sports provided a turnaround in his attitude. He began playing wheelchair basketball and, after only two years, won a bronze medal at the Paralympic World Championships. The young Australian continued to dominate the sport.

After medaling in a number of basketball events, Alcott turned to wheelchair tennis, where he was named one of the top five juniors in the world. He made a big impression when he achieved the distinction of setting the world record for the longest continuous game of wheelchair tennis—24 hours. His feat brought attention to the sport and also raised money for two charities.

Dylan won double Paralympic gold medals in Rio and four Olympic golds all-around in two sports: tennis and basketball. He has won 15 Grand Slam tennis tournaments before his retirement from professional sport in 2022. Alcott also co-founded a start-up for disability and accessibility training. He now travels the world as a motivational speaker. In 2022, he was named Australian of the Year and made an officer of the Order of Australia.

My Father

My father contracted polio in his preteen years and spent six months in an iron lung in one of the major hospitals over 400 miles away from his parents and young brother. He overheard a doctor once say in a noisy corridor outside his hospital room, "*Sh*. There is a young boy dying in there."

What my father endured in his younger years inspired him to achieve what many can only dream of. I still marvel at his tenacity and endurance to this day. He has also been an inspiration to me for his never-fail positive attitude and the aura of resounding love that surrounded him.

He was always smiling and gracious even in the darkest moments. In the last few years of his life, the palliative staff at the facility he was in affectionately called him "Smiley." No matter what pain and discomfort, no matter what restrictions he had to endure, he would smile. When his vocabulary went, he spoke with his pleasant facial expressions and his ever-present smile.

Dad showed me how to live and how to die. His legacy is profound. My father was living proof that the impact you make on Earth is enduring. He lives on. Individuals like him continue to live on within us. That is the tremendous impact each person can create.

Your Own Inspirations

Search the internet and find your own heroes who have conquered adversity to achieve great things. There are plenty of other celebrities whose stories can inspire. Join their fan base and follow their careers. Read their biographies and enjoy shows about their lives and their pursuits. Keep your own record of their accomplishments by making a scrapbook. Choose inspirations from your country or your favorite sport.

Don't forget about heroes from other fields of endeavor as well. Think about scientist and author Stephen Hawking, who, despite being paralyzed by motor neuron disease, profoundly influenced the world with his thinking and writing about the origins of the universe.

Learn more about Nan Davis, who, despite being paralyzed from the ribs down, eventually walked across the stage to get her college diploma and begin a career in education. This was a tribute to her own determination and breakthroughs from a visionary professor in biomedical engineering who pioneered advances in computer-controlled electric stimulation.

Discover Teddy Pendergrass, a recording artist with quadriplegia. And, of course, no list of inspirational heroes would be complete without baseball player Lou Gehrig, whose name was synonymous with the disease now called ALS.

Legacy

It's only natural to think about what you will leave behind when you are gone. If you've worked through your grief and other emotions, you can start thinking about what your legacy will be. I'll discuss this more in Chapter 8, but for now, here are the basics.

A legacy takes many forms. The primary one is memories. Those who are left behind will have reasons to remember you—your worth as a person, your example, the things you've said and done. To help preserve those memories, they will have photos and videos of you. Don't be hesitant to let them add to their store of souvenirs. Even if you don't like how you look, they will treasure the memento simply because you have been an important part of their lives.

Another way to preserve your memory is to contribute to an organization that helps others. It can be any one that raises money or awareness for a cause, but you may want to choose one that relates to your specific situation.

For example, if a drunk driver caused an accident that made you paraplegic, you might want to support the work of Mothers Against Drunk Driving. If you were injured by an explosion or bullet while serving in the armed forces, you could give time or money to the

Wounded Warrior Project. There are also foundations that support research into cures for devastating diseases like Parkinson's, multiple sclerosis, and heart disease. Raising money for one of them is a much-needed contribution that will do some good for others. If ecology has been one of your causes, you can request that your loved ones plant a tree as a memorial after you're gone. Anything you can do to help others is a worthy legacy.

Just spending time with friends, family members, and loved ones is another way to pass on a legacy. Share what you've learned through your life and encourage others to make the most of their time on Earth as well. Pass on skills you've learned, passions you've pursued, or art you've created. Young people will especially appreciate your time and attention and make it part of their lives. Then, they can pass it on in their turn so your legacy continues down through the generations.

Of course, considering your legacy will raise difficult emotions. You may have regrets for things you never got to do or overwhelming sadness at the thought of your life ending. However, you may find comfort and peace in your religious or philosophical beliefs. You can gather your loved ones and the resources you need to prepare. They can help you meet your needs at this time and be with you as you approach the end of your life's journey.

Your personality, your family, your beliefs, your age, your support networks (both personal and medical), the circumstances of your diagnosis, and your culture will all be factors in how you face the rest of your life and what may happen afterward.

It would be presumptuous for me to suggest how you should approach this transition. Just remember that death is a part of life that comes to everyone. Each person now alive will someday go through what you are facing.

Key Takeaways

- Some trauma creates a transformative grief in which your life changes significantly. When you have a diagnosis or prognosis that brings you to an assessment of your own life, you feel grief. But that grief can transform you by how you react to it. You are not your diagnosis, and it doesn't have to define you.

- Professionals, including your family doctor, therapists, rehabilitation specialists, and hospice workers are part of your support system. Your family members will be part of your support team, but they, too, will be affected by grief. Having that outside support will make your journey less arduous.

- You need mental and emotional endurance as part of your mindset to overcome prolonged grief regarding your condition. You'll experience setbacks, but you should strive to keep them in perspective and work your way past them.

- Role models can inspire you to develop a positive mindset. Their struggles and triumphs will give you something to celebrate and aspire to.

Section 2:

Preparing for Recovery

Chapter 6:

Emotions That Consume

Rainbows

Imaginary; Dreamy; Colorful

Do you question that person in the mirror?

Trauma can change your personality—sometimes temporarily but also on a more permanent basis. Emotions and belief systems are central to your personality. Profound and tragic circumstances and experiences can change the way you perceive yourself and how you interact with others. So, if you don't recognize the person in the mirror or can't comprehend the changes within you, this chapter may give you the answer.

Emotions, Thoughts, and Feelings

You may remember from the second book in this series that emotions, thoughts, and feelings are part of human comprehension—they're what make you *you*! Your frame of reference is *how* and *why* you react to every stimulus around you. Here's a quick review of what you need to know about them.

Emotions are physical, biochemical reactions to what happens around you. The circumstances you find around you are the stimuli that you respond to with emotions. The most common or basic emotions that all people in the world share are anger, disgust, fear, happiness, sadness, and surprise. There are a variety of stimuli that cause these emotions. For example, an attack by a wild animal or a mugger produces fear, while, as you know all too well, the death of a loved one causes sadness. These reactions are automatic ones that you can't control. They're instinctive and come from the unconscious, the part of your mind that operates without you realizing it.

Thoughts are different, but they are influenced by your emotions. Your mind is like an ever-evolving database that you add to every time you experience something—an emotion, a stimulus, a thought, an event, or a piece of information. Ever since you were an infant, everything has been added to that database and evaluated and recalculated according to that input. Your thoughts are based on your emotional response to a stimulus. The emotion of fear results in thoughts of how you can escape from a threat. The emotion of sadness leads to thoughts that may or may not reflect reality.

Feelings are the expression of your emotions and thoughts about what is occurring or has occurred. All this will determine your behavior. That mugger who threatened you brought forth the emotion of fear and the thought that you must escape. Your feeling afterward may be that you are a coward for not fighting back. Even though this isn't realistic or true, you have the feeling anyway. Your behavior may change enough that you take a martial arts class in response to your emotions, thoughts, and feelings.

Trauma Changes You

Your grief has been overwhelming and traumatic. That affects you significantly. It can change not only your emotions but also your personality. These changes can be for the worse or the better, but they will be noticeable to your friends, family, and loved ones. They'll be aware that you've changed even if you're not.

Your nervous system can change in one of two ways: through high arousal or low arousal. If your nerves are too stimulated (called hyperarousal), you can become overstimulated, which means that you'll become more wary of incoming stimuli. You can be easily startled and jumpy or more anxious than usual. If you have low arousal (called hypoarousal), you can feel numb and detached, leading you to become less engaged or responsive. Either of these outcomes will change your behavior.

You can also develop unhealthy coping mechanisms. They may have served you well when the trauma was fresh, but as time goes on, they can become habits unrelated to it. For example, you might try to deal with your overwhelming emotions by avoiding reminders of the deceased. So, you change your route to work so as not to drive by their house or a park where you often jogged together. You might even turn to substance abuse.

You've probably heard of "survivor's guilt." It's when you feel guilt or shame because your loved one is dead while you are physically unhurt. Soldiers returning from war often have this problem if they have seen close buddies die. If a loved one dies in a natural disaster, you might beat yourself up for not having been there to protect them. It can be irrational, but that doesn't make it feel any less real.

Trauma can also change your basic beliefs about the world. You may come to view the world as a hostile and dangerous place and retreat from society. You might develop a pessimistic outlook on life. You can also easily develop unhealthy views of yourself, such as "I am powerless" or "I am broken."

When a loved one has died, you could also have a sense of abandonment or rejection. You know that this person who has been close to you will never come back. Moving ahead, you may have difficulty forming and maintaining relationships because you fear suffering another loss.

What Psychology Says

Psychological theory and practice can offer a lot of insights into how your emotions, thoughts, and feelings work when you have experienced a tragic loss. Because so many of your responses are instinctual or unconscious, you probably don't realize how strongly they are influencing you.

Projection

When you're having undesirable emotions and feelings, instead of dealing with them directly, you may project them onto someone else.

For example, Marla may come to resent Janelle for being so close to her husband, Ed, whom she works with. She knows that she should be nice to Janelle for her husband's sake. But, over time, she begins to realize that Janelle doesn't like her either. Whenever they both show up at an office party or company picnic, Marla thinks Janelle is being snippy with her, especially if Ed is nearby. Marla tells Ed that she has really tried to get along with Janelle, but she thinks the reason she doesn't like Janelle is that Janelle doesn't like her. Marla has projected her feelings of dislike and resentment onto Janelle.

Consuming negative emotions that linger can become so undesirable that you can project emotionally onto someone or something to avoid or justify the emotions you have. You don't recognize that that's what's happening, however, since your reactions are unconscious, buried deep in your mind.

Recovery From Negative Emotions, Thoughts, and Feelings

You might not even comprehend that your feelings are irrational. You may just have a sense that there is something you need to get off your chest or that the person you have projected your feelings onto has always been that way. You might say that laughing children have always irritated you, rather than realizing you are projecting your uncomfortable feelings onto them.

It can be difficult for someone to realize that they are projecting because so much of it is unconscious or subconscious. Other people may see it and draw conclusions about the cause. They may even bring this insight to the person who is suffering emotionally. But they're not likely to be believed. Perhaps telling the person who has been projecting will only make things worse and provoke even more negative emotions and behavior.

You may have heard that the first step in psychological recovery is admitting you have a problem, and that's true! That's not so easy when you think that it's another person causing your feelings or that it's all due to an adverse or problematic stimulus. But ask yourself: Who would want to be controlled by negative emotions? That's an easier question to answer.

Sadness, anger, hate, jealousy, envy, resentment, suspicion, and revenge are all emotions that can control your feelings and behavior. In fact, any projected emotions can be difficult to identify if you haven't determined the root causes of them. If you don't proactively try to remedy your projection, your sense of self and your personality can be damaged.

Red Flags That Signal You Need Help

Realizing that you are projecting your emotions is one sign that your negative reactions and emotions need to be addressed. Your changed behavior and thought patterns resulting from trauma can really be psychological projections and indicate that you need to seek help.

If someone's loved one has been murdered, for example, their inner emotional battle can be prolonged and persistent. There will often be anger; in fact, it can be pure hatred toward the person or people who have taken the life of their loved one. This emotion can control them.

The anger and fury caused by a tragedy—even one that may have occurred a considerable time ago—may still influence their life.

Then, when this same person has an ordinarily nontraumatic experience such as a personal encounter or a certain visual stimulus, their reaction is likely to be anything but rational. For example, if one of their friends mentions a news story about rising crime rates, they might go ballistic and yell at that friend. If the loved one had been a child, and they see a playground of happy children in a park, their emotions may get out of control. *How dare they be happy*, they may think. *The world is fucked up, and they don't even realize it!*

An innocent person bears the brunt of your wrath, resentment, dislike, or hatred when you have not recovered effectively from your traumatic experience. You will have become an angry, resentful, spiteful person who is untrusting and suspicious of anyone and everything. This is how an individual can change because they have experienced trauma.

Psychological projection is a defense mechanism. You may project your own feelings or qualities onto someone else, often unconsciously. This allows you to deny the knowledge that your emotions are the source of negative feelings or behavior. It's a way to cope with internal conflicts and anxiety. Instead of dealing with your feelings, you cast them onto others, allowing you to avoid anxiety or another unpleasant reaction.

Projection isn't always a sign of cognitive dysfunction, but when it becomes a persistent, problematic reaction to everyday events, it can be a sign that you need help. Therapy and self-reflection can help you understand the underlying issues and promote personal growth and emotional awareness.

Unbeknownst to me at the time, I've personally changed through traumatic experiences. For many years after the tragic death of my wife, several aspects of my personality changed dramatically. Anger and resentment bubbled under the surface. I became very emotionally distressed by relatively benign stimuli. I did not like the person I had become.

Thankfully, this process does not need to last forever.

Through self-analysis—and often with professional guidance—I was able to see the flaws in my perceptions, take ownership of the reasons for my personality changes, and bring about an emotional awareness that brought me out of the dark. Emotional awareness and emotional growth are not just check-the-box exercises that make everything all better.

Two decades later, I still have regrets and long for my wife. I'm just not controlled by negative, irrational, or distorted emotions like I was before.

The Next Steps

Exactly where are you in your grief journey? During the grieving process, there will always be circumstances or events that will call forth raw emotion. Often, emotional hurdles appear, sometimes years after your tragic loss, that can cause sadness and anger but also resentment, envy, and other problematic reactions. You may think these are just normal reactions to change and to life in general. Really, though, they can be signs that you need to take the next steps toward healing your grief.

Many people can continue in life bitter, envious, condescending, hateful, and negative. They don't realize what is driving their emotions, or they relentlessly search for the reasons they feel this way. They want to justify their feelings and behavior.

Perhaps your personality changes or projected emotions have been brought to your attention by a family member or a close friend. You yourself may be tired of how you relate to other people and view the world. You may not like how you respond to ordinary stimuli. When you're fed up with your reactions to your life and other people are fed up with you and how you're behaving, it can be a catalyst that will move you into a phase where you can change your life.

You've come to such a moment when you're asking: Why have I been acting this way? Why did I say such a hurtful thing to someone who was only trying to help me? Why have I changed? And what can I do about these things?

And the big one: Who is that person looking back out from my mirror?

If you are asking yourself these questions and having these feelings, it's really positive comprehension. You've realized that something needs to change, and that thing is you.

Your distress has been caused by unresolved emotions from your tragic loss. It's been driven by irrationality and distorted thoughts and belief systems that have affected what has happened in your life and how you've responded. But there is real hope for positive change if you are ready and willing to look in that mirror and see yourself as you are, even if you don't particularly like the person looking back at you yet.

But don't despair—there is hope! You've taken the first step by admitting that you have a problem. The next step? Being proactive and committed to change.

Key Takeaways

- Trauma can change aspects of your personality. The severe, prolonged trauma that you experience in reaction to a devastating loss can seriously affect your emotions, thoughts, and even your behavior.

- Certain emotions can be so profound and consuming that you can start projecting emotions onto someone else. Projection is a psychological defense mechanism designed to shield you from feeling the emotions you project.

- When you do not know or like the reflection in your mirror, it's time for you to resolve to change. There is hope!

Chapter 7:

Missing Pieces of the Puzzle

Moon and Stars

Dreamy; Wondrous; Infinite

Are you at an impasse? When life has progressed but there is such a change in your character that you avoid your reflection and hate your life, it's time to become a little vulnerable and explore the reason you have reached this point in life.

Your State of Being

Delving deeper into what's been occurring in your life since your tragic loss can uncover missing positive qualities within you that will aid your recovery. No matter where you are with your grief or how long it has been since your loved one passed, there comes a time to reassemble the lost pieces.

How long has it been since you experienced the tragic event? A year? Multiple years? You may have been desperately trying to recover to regain your composure or your purpose in life. You may even believe you have restored your sense of self. But then the roller-coaster ride of emotions just never seems to stop, so there are still times when you exhibit raw emotions and irrational behavior that disturb and concern you.

Triggers

Memories can have two extremes. There are enlightening and purposeful ones that create hope and happiness. There are also memories of trauma, which can be completely torturous and soul-destroying.

Say there's been some time since your loss occurred. You've achieved something like stability for a little while and maybe even started to reconnect with your social circle. Then, all of a sudden, for no apparent reason, you begin to tremble and shake. You feel weak and nauseous. You may feel paralyzed. You have to get away, back to a safe place if you can find one. You experience a rapid, uncontrollable downturn in your emotional state.

You may be reacting to a trigger.

Triggers are things that remind you of your loss. But they're not just ordinary reminders. A trigger can send you back to the time when your loved one died or blindside you with a vivid recurrence of the traumatic event. You relive it as if it were happening in the present moment. You might break down in public, sobbing uncontrollably. You could have realistic nightmares when you sleep that leave you shaken when you wake.

The trigger doesn't have to be something big and obvious. It could be something that no one else would notice. For example, a scene in a movie or TV show may remind you that you experienced a tragedy. It could even be a comedy show. Just something about one of the actors or a joke they make could remind you of your loved one and bring on the emotions you thought you'd buried. A sight, a scent, a sound—

anything that viscerally reminds you of the person you've lost—can bring on this vivid sense of recall.

The sight of children playing on the playground or in the schoolyard, a young family enjoying time together at the beach, park, or a sports event—any one of these scenarios can create a negative state of mind to some degree. You could be instantly and intensely sad, angry, or envious. The emotion could be fleeting, or it could overcome you with an intense emotional breakdown that makes you feel that you are reliving the experience all over again.

Service personnel returning from a war zone are especially vulnerable to triggers that bring them back to scenes they witnessed or participated in. It could be the death of comrades, being pinned down by enemy fire, or the smell and the sounds of combat. The trauma they experienced was so impactful that certain stimuli can make the person feel like they are right back there among all that horror.

You might have been at a movie when a scene of a car backfiring played out on the screen. You could have noticed an ex-service person sitting near you ducking for cover because they instantly had a reaction that reminded them of an experience they had in combat. This example is a little stereotypical, but it's what a basic trigger looks and feels like.

News reports of a tragedy like the one that took your loved one are a common trigger. Any media coverage of a suicide, traffic accident, murder, or abduction can cause intense psychological pain. If this is what you experienced in the past, the trigger could cause you to relive the moment, bringing on the feeling that the tragedy is happening all over again.

Response to a trigger can cause a major setback in your journey to healing. Once you've experienced it, you may retreat from the world, fearing that the traumatic reaction may recur.

Emotional triggers are common. You are not deficient or going mad in any way. These are simply stimuli that provoke your memory. This can be controlled by creating emotional awareness. Many people try unsuccessfully to live with this torment, which can have dire consequences for them when they are trying to continue with their lives.

Emotional Awareness

Knowing your triggers is important, but you will need professional help to uncover them and deal with them. You can't just make the emotional meltdowns go away by saying "I was triggered," and you can't avoid the triggers forever. That will make your life even more limited and unsatisfying. You can keep encountering stimuli that didn't trigger you before but do now. Unexpectedly, you'll be right back in the middle of your traumatic memories.

A mental health professional can help you determine what your triggers are and how they pull you into a downward spiral. It's not a matter of simply eliminating the trigger. It isn't like a hypnotic suggestion. It's something real out in the world that you won't be able to avoid forever. Also, you can't simply erase the memories that your triggers conjure up. That's just not realistic.

You should also learn what the bodily and mental effects of encountering your trigger are. That way, when your palms get sweaty and your knees begin to shake, you'll know what's happening—that you're in the grip of a powerful memory. With the proper help, you can understand your triggers and their effects, as well as prepare yourself for when you next encounter them and their residual effects.

How do you keep these effects from happening? To an extent, you can't. Emotions associated with certain traumas are very powerful. But you can learn to tone down the residual effects they have on you, lessening how often they occur and how much they affect you.

Being prepared and emotionally equipped to deal with triggers is key. Seeking professional help from a trauma specialist is the best step you can take. It's a positive decision that will help you in getting your life back. The life skills, strategies, and techniques you learn through therapy will greatly assist you in progressing with your life in a more positive way.

Your Team

If you broke your leg, would you be expected to just put up with it and hope it gets better on its own? Of course not. You would need the services of a number of professionals to help you.

The doctor or emergency department personnel would see to your immediate needs. The radiologist would use medical imaging to determine the extent of your injury. Medical staff and technicians would know the procedures required to set the broken leg. An orthopedic surgeon and operating room personnel might be required if the break is a particularly bad one that needs to be pinned. A pharmacist could fill the doctors' prescriptions for pain meds. Other staff would work with you to determine your mobility needs, as well as after-care and the monitoring of your condition. Rehab alone could involve several other professions—physiotherapists and occupational therapists, for example.

It's the same deal with recovery from grief. You need many kinds of help from a variety of people. Each of them has something special to offer you.

Consulting with your GP is the first step. They will help to develop a mental health plan that will likely involve referrals to mental health professionals who will assist you in working through the difficult changes in your life. They could recommend a psychologist, a psychiatrist, or a trauma counselor. You could need to make one or more appointments that your doctor will refer you to in order to aid your recovery.

You may need to see more than one kind of mental health helper. You could need a psychologist to assess your condition and refer you to a psychiatrist if you need medications. The trauma counselor will work with you to address the cause of your trauma, what's keeping you stuck in grief, and how to get out of its grasp.

You will very likely have apprehension about seeing a mental health professional. Revealing yourself in terms of sensitive matters, emotional disclosure, and painful discussion is very difficult. Reliving your moments of distress and breakdowns will feel difficult at first.

However, to prevent being consumed and controlled by the emotions of your trauma needs positive intervention. That is why you need to go to these appointments—to gain emotional relief and to work toward recovery.

Don't be daunted by the stereotyped versions of these professions you see in the movies and on TV. Any negative beliefs you have of these helpers—that they are cold, uninvolved, or likely to confuse you with psychological jargon—are mistaken. They have years of training and experience in helping people just like you. Take my word for it. The decision to get help can transform you. You have nothing to lose and plenty to gain!

You shouldn't forget that there are nonprofessional sources of help as well. You can get some kinds of support from bereavement groups and even family and friends. They may not understand the depth of your grief or why you are suffering so much. Some of them may expect you to "snap out of it" or "choose happiness," but others will be sympathetic, give a shoulder to cry on and a hand to reach out to, and just listen. Such people are to be treasured. They may not be able to relieve your suffering completely, but they may be able to help if you let them.

Expectations of Therapy

What can you get from allowing a trauma therapist to help you?

First, there is emotional relief. You will be in a safe place, in all meanings of the word. The therapeutic environment is designed so you can openly express what your life has been like. They will initially focus on developing a comfortable working relationship with you. Their body language and mannerisms will help you feel connected and confident enough to express your feelings without reservation. You will gain confidence and momentum as self-discovery materializes.

Therapy will likely be difficult and upsetting at first. The therapist will initially need to know what has occurred in your life. But they are skilled at interpersonal interaction and will be able to create a safe environment for self-expression and disclosure. Your appointments will lead you to greater understanding. The professional relationship between you and the therapist is crucial for effectiveness in treatment. They will know this, and they will never reveal to anyone what you say in the privacy of your appointments.

Your therapist will understand the difficulties and heartache the process will cause. Your emotional needs and your well-being are foremost in their mind. Since they will ask you to reveal personal details, they will be sensitive to your need for reassurance and empathy. Along your journey, they will make adjustments to your treatment plan as needed to reflect the progress or setbacks you encounter. As you progress, they will stay with you every step of the way. It's all meant to guide you to emotional awareness.

Preparing for Therapy

Your therapy will go more smoothly if you have a written list of questions and facts to communicate with your therapist when you first meet them. Start by noting down the symptoms you've been having and how long you've been experiencing them. Include physical symptoms as well as emotional ones. They can help your counselor determine the extent of your prolonged grief and what needs to be done to alleviate those symptoms. For example, if you're experiencing migraines or backaches, the therapist will probably introduce you to relaxation techniques that can relieve the tension you're holding in your body. Then, you can go on to resolve any tension that exists in your mind.

Knowing your personal and family history can be beneficial in your treatment. Your therapist will want to know about any other significant traumas you've encountered. Say that you're going to therapy because you've recently received a terminal diagnosis. Your therapist will want to know if you have had other major stressors in your life such as going through a divorce, losing your job, or even moving into a new house. These circumstances can complicate your grief and your therapy.

Of course, you should let your counselor know of any medical information they may need as they plan your treatment. This can make a difference if they want to prescribe medication. Knowing what medicines you're already taking can make a difference in what meds they give you and what doses they prescribe. Take along a complete list, including the dosages you're on. Include any vitamins and herbal supplements that you take.

Finally, take a list of questions you want to ask. You may want to know whether they think you have prolonged grief. Other typical questions include what kind of therapy they specialize in and approximately how long they think treatment will last. If they prescribe medication, ask about any side effects you might experience. Ask if they can recommend any support groups that could give you another perspective and encouragement.

Your therapist will have questions for you, too, so you should be prepared to answer them:

- How long has it been since your trauma occurred?

- Are you keeping up with work, household chores, and relationships?

- Have you seen a therapist before? How did that go?

- Are you having trouble eating or sleeping?

- How often do you think about your trauma?

- Have you ever had disturbing thoughts of self-harm?

It may be uncomfortable but still do your best to answer their questions honestly. Your therapy will be more effective if your counselor knows as much as possible about you.

Most of all, it's important for you to engage with the therapy. Go to all your appointments and do any exercises your therapist gives you to try at home. If you don't feel up to going to your appointment, get someone else to drive you there. Or ask your therapist if they can do a video or telephone appointment. If you're getting medication, you'll probably have to see the doctor in person. Most of them won't give you a prescription without seeing you in the office.

Types of Therapy

There are different types of therapy that can help with addressing the trauma of grief. Your therapist may use various techniques as you go through your journey from grief to healing. Here's a look at some of them.

Narrative Exposure Therapy

As a way to reclaim your identity and story, narrative exposure therapy centers on assisting you in creating an account of how your trauma is currently impacting your life. Everyone has an internalized story of their life. Yours includes a lot about your loss, your trauma, and your grief. It has become part of your core identity.

In this form of therapy, you create a story for yourself that encompasses not only your grief but also the other aspects of your life. It integrates your experiences from the traumatic to the positive. They are all part of the story of you, and you need to remember that. Narrative exposure therapy facilitates compiling a chronological story of your life that helps your therapist develop a mental health plan that will help you create a new story. You don't lose the memory of your trauma, but it ceases to be the main event in your story.

Cognitive Behavior Therapy and Cognitive Processing Therapy

These two techniques are among the most common therapies that assist with trauma recovery, and they are both very effective. Both are recommended for use in healing from traumatic events.

Cognitive behavior therapy (CBT) and cognitive processing therapy are based on the premise that thoughts and behaviors are interwoven. When your thoughts are distorted and your belief systems are irrational, they influence your human reckoning and memory. These thoughts and beliefs can be understood and challenged to facilitate behavioral improvements.

This therapy allows a client to identify, assess, and modify negative perceptions and actions that result in unnecessary distress. It can include fostering your problem-solving skills, developing confidence in your own abilities, and facing your negative emotions. You work together with your therapist to create a treatment plan that will address your personal circumstances.

Prolonged Exposure Therapy

Prolonged exposure therapy is a technique related to CBT and is sometimes used in conjunction with it. This technique uses systematic desensitization through prolonged exposure to stressful trauma cues, leading to the alleviation of your symptoms. You don't avoid your triggers, and there is no expectation of them being eliminated from your life. They exist and will continue to exist, but a structured plan and exercises such as journaling create gradual exposure to triggers that can bring about a different response.

Exposure to the triggers is difficult for those suffering from prolonged grief, but the therapist creates a safe space to confront them. These grounding techniques will enable you to learn that these stimuli do not pose a danger and do not need to be avoided. This is a process that is monitored, tweaked, and discussed as needed to ensure that it's effective.

Relaxation Training

Relaxation training is a CBT tool that can help reduce the stress and anxiety you're feeling because of your continuing trauma. It's often used in conjunction with cognitive restructuring and exposure therapy, but it can be used on its own for short-term coping with grief. It's designed to short-circuit your body's stress response and replace it with a relaxation response that includes slower breathing, reduced heart rate, and lower blood pressure.

Components of relaxation training can include progressive muscle relaxation, breathing exercises, guided imagery, biofeedback, and self-hypnosis. Meditation and yoga can also be helpful. You can practice these techniques on your own or while you're discussing your trauma with your therapist. It's best if you try these practices under the supervision of a mental health professional.

Eye Movement Desensitization and Reprocessing

Eye movement desensitization and reprocessing (EMDR) was originally developed to treat various kinds of trauma, and it is now used in the treatment of PGD as well. You experience the stimulation of eye movements while processing distressing memories and emotions. If there are traumatic aspects to your grief, such as losing your loved one to an accident or at the hands of another person, EMDR is a therapy your mental health professional may consider. EMDR taps into the natural adaptive power of the brain to make a traumatic memory less likely to trouble you.

Finding the Missing Pieces

When you think about the long-lasting effects of trauma, you can find it difficult to look into the metaphoric mirror. You may not like who you see there, or you may not even recognize yourself. You may hate how you react and how you behave, and you almost certainly hate what has brought you to this point. The emotions that have consumed you have severely affected your behavior and changed aspects of your personality.

You're still the same person—you're just missing a few pieces of the jigsaw puzzle that is your life. But it's a beautiful jigsaw puzzle. You can imagine what will appear when all the pieces fit together again. You just need to find those missing pieces.

Professional guidance can help you find the missing pieces and reintegrate them into the larger picture. You don't need to go through this process alone. There are great prospects for a new life for you. Do what it takes to recreate your life with the beauty you once had. You can find it again with some time and training from a mental health practitioner.

Key Takeaways

- You may believe you have restored your sense of self, but there are times of raw emotion or irrational behavior that you find troubling and concerning.

- Emotions can change aspects of your personality.

- A trigger is a specific stimulus or experience that provokes the memory of your trauma so that you relive the experience, feelings, or behavior. Emotional triggers can be particularly terrifying and debilitating.

- Emotional awareness is necessary for your healing to progress.

- Professional help will likely be necessary to assist you in putting the missing pieces of the puzzle back together.

- You owe it to yourself to try getting help. You have so much to gain and nothing to lose except your crippling grief.

Chapter 8:

The Power of Legacy

Human Togetherness

Belonging; Love; Acceptance

The power of legacy knows no limits! The legacy of the departed and the legacy that you intend for them can be lessons to live on; they can be an example of existence. The positive impact of your loved one's life is a guide for those who remain. Legacy can be powerful. Legacy can move you to another realm of deeper understanding and purpose. Feel that power and watch it transform you!

The Meaning of Legacy

What is a legacy?

At first, you may think of a legacy as something material that a person bequeaths to others in their will. People pass along money, of course, but also property and possessions. If they die suddenly without a will, the state takes over and apportions their assets to their family.

Often, we hear about the legacy that a sports star like Jesse Owens, a singer-songwriter like Jimmy Buffet, or a scientist like Marie Curie leaves. And it's true that they do leave behind great accomplishments, art, or learning passed down to future generations. We marvel at their achievements and the positive impact they've had on other people or society at large. Thinking about their life and works can leave you inspired, uplifted, and hopeful. They can inspire you to be your best self.

But money and fame are not the only legacy a person leaves. Even if they're relative unknowns, they leave the sum total of how they lived, what they knew, their values, and the experiences they've shared. The time you've had with the deceased, the lessons you've learned from them, and the good times you enjoyed together are parts of their legacy that you can treasure forever.

These legacies are just as real as monetary ones and, in many ways, even more valuable. Money can only last for a while. Property can be sold. Possessions can be lost. The profound effects of a person's life are a more lasting legacy, memories that you can call on at any time.

What's important to know is that every person we know and each person whose death we grieve leaves behind a legacy. Every person's life creates some kind of impact. If you mourn a life that has departed, there is a legacy waiting to be realized and celebrated.

What is the legacy that a deceased friend, loved one, or family member created? And how do you celebrate and honor it? Start determining this by asking yourself the following questions:

- How has my loved one positively impacted my life?

- How am I richer for having had this person in my life?

- What are the lessons my loved one has taught or instilled in me?

- What were their positive traits?

- What were their achievements?

- How has my life been made more fruitful and significant by having this person in it?

- How can the way my loved one lived their life guide me in mine?

It can be a beautiful, powerful moment when you reflect on how your loved one has influenced you. As you think about your relationship, you may discover aspects of their life that you had not previously recognized. Allow everything you hold dear about them to influence the rest of yours. Their inspiration can cancel out any negativity that you feel. You can give their existence additional purpose and meaning as you live out their legacy.

Your State of Mind

You do need to go through a period of grieving for a life that has been lost. But though your loss has been profound and your grief profound and prolonged, you have the opportunity to renew and redefine yourself after the death. Once the negative emotions you've suffered are no longer so all-consuming, the person's legacy can inspire you. In the first book in this series, I referred to this moment as an awakening.

Developing a positive attitude toward the person's legacy will take time. It can't be rushed. When you are finally ready to think back on your time together, you can decide how to celebrate and honor that legacy. Think of the person's legacy as a way for you to reconnect with their life—and with your own. You redefine your life by living through loss and making peace with the reality of it.

After you have been able to grieve, within your own timeline and from your frame of reference, it's time to search for the way forward. Think about it like this: *If I remain in misery and heartache, two lives miss out on life. Would my loved one want their legacy to be one of sorrow and despair?*

When you think in terms of legacy, you can use this as a catalyst for positive change within yourself, and you'll be amazed at the transformation. Your loved one's shortcomings fade. Trivial considerations lose their power. You can gain perspective on what really matters. Your traumatic experience can make you appreciate the small things in life again. You can get great joy from the simple things that many people take for granted.

You can find yourself becoming more accepting, more loving, and contributing more to the life within and around you. You redefine yourself—all because of what you have lost and what you've gained from your loved one. You can live a life that is not restricted by the grief you felt when you lost them. The beautiful life your loved one has enabled you to enjoy—that was their legacy. Through their death, they have breathed new life into you.

The Legacy of a Life Too Short

You've heard it said that when a child dies, a part of the parent or other family members dies too. You likely have heard this sentiment from the person experiencing this anguish and pain. But a part of them doesn't die. It is just lost for a time.

Even a young life taken too soon has a legacy to share. The trauma of a stillborn baby or a miscarriage has a devastating emotional impact on the parents who had celebrated the addition to their family. But the death of early life, even before it had a chance to live, can also provide a legacy for you.

In time, this trauma can profoundly influence and encourage you to live a productive and full life. A miscarried or stillborn baby may not have had the opportunity to breathe air, but they most certainly can breathe life into you. Live your life because of them. Embrace every good thing and seek fulfillment each day simply because that small life wasn't able to.

Yes, you do change through experiencing trauma, but you can also reach a place of emotional strength. You may never get over grieving the loss, but you will eventually be able to reach a state of mind where you can consider the legacy of that small life—the anticipation of waiting to welcome them, the joy in discovering more about yourself as a parent, and the bond you will always feel. Let that be the legacy that carries on their memory.

Honoring Your Loved One

There are many ways to honor your loved one and remember their legacy. When you think of creating a memorial, you usually think of a funeral or other service and a grave marker. Having those is important. But when you suffer from prolonged grief, those memorials are likely receding into the past. You may feel the need for an additional memorial now that you have made progress on your grief journey. It's never too late to have some special remembrance for the departed. For all you know, others may be suffering in silence, too, caught up in their own prolonged grief.

What's important is that you choose a memorial that reflects the life and personality of your loved one. It can be a source of comfort and healing for you and anyone else who loved them. It doesn't have to be big or expensive, though it can be if you have the means to do that. Instead, it should be a source of remembrance and celebration of the life that was lived.

Here are some types of memorials you could consider.

Memorial Ceremony

You may think that just because the funeral happened, there's no sense in having another memorial service or ceremony. You can hold the memorial on the anniversary of the death or another occasion you choose, such as the first day of spring. Invite people who knew the person. Tell them that they'll have an opportunity to celebrate the person in a special, meaningful way. You can ask people to share stories, music, or photos. You can light candles in sequence around a circle to symbolize the spirit of the person being remembered.

Memorial Space

Set aside a space in your home as a place to think of your friend, family member, or other loved one. Place a bench by your flower garden and go there when you want to contemplate their life. Plant their favorite flowers in the garden. Reserve a space in your house or apartment to keep photos on display. Plant a tree in their memory to symbolize hope, renewal, and life.

Donations

It's always the right time to remember your loved one by donating money or time in their name to their favorite cause or organization. Think of it as a way of continuing their legacy and extending it into the future. You could donate to Mothers Against Drunk Driving if they died in a traffic accident or a victim's advocacy group if their life was cut short by crime. Public works projects such as parks and civic buildings often allow people to donate a bench or an engraved brick in memory of someone who has passed. You can visit the site whenever you feel a need to renew your relationship.

Artwork

Create a drawing, painting, sculpture, or other artwork that symbolizes your relationship and display it in your home. If you aren't artistically talented, you could commission a work of art based on one of your photos. Display the piece in the space in your home you've dedicated to your loved one's memory.

Online Memorial

Create a blog, website, or social media page for your loved one. Include pictures and an account of their life. Add poems, quotations, artwork, and testimonials from other people. Invite others who were connected to your friend, family member, or significant other to add to it. Return to the page as often as you need to refresh your pleasant memories.

Personalized Items

You could have a piece of jewelry inscribed with the name and dates of your loved one. Or select a saying they loved or a Bible verse that held special meaning for them. You can even have a T-shirt created with a meaningful quotation or symbol on it. Wear it whenever you feel a need to be close to your friend, family member, or loved one.

Rituals of Remembrance

Remembering your loved one is important to you and part of keeping their legacy alive. I talked about this kind of ritual in the first book in this series—you may want to refer to that book if you have it or get yourself a copy to assist in your journey through loss and grief.

A ritual or private ceremony can be a very powerful way to remember your friend, loved one, or family member and to honor their legacy. Pick a time that feels right to you, whether that be the person's birthday, the date of their death, or a significant occasion such as a wedding anniversary, a holiday, or a religious observance. You may find these occasions very difficult because they bring up memories.

Let those memories be honored and celebrated with a private ceremony that brings you comfort and peace. By symbolizing and honoring their life, you can create a closeness, a connection—a statement and action of complete love and appreciation for having had this person in your life.

Do what you feel is right for you. Here's a ritual that helps me in remembrance of my father.

I have a small urn filled with my father's ashes on the top shelf of a bookcase in my sitting room. Next to the urn, I have placed three framed photos of my dad that hold special significance for me. I bought a nice candle.

On special anniversaries, I go into the living room and light it. I talk as if my dad were standing next to me. I say how much I love him, how special he was to me, and how much I miss him. As I am speaking, I place one hand on the urn, and with the other, I caress his face in one of the photos. Then I look at the candle for a while before blowing it out.

This is a very powerful remembrance that feels good for me. It's a way of continuing his presence in my life and my love for him.

Writing a letter to your loved one is another time-honored way of embracing their memory. I've recommended this form of emotional release in therapy with my clients and have done it myself as well. I use this technique to express thoughts, feelings, desires, regrets, hopes, and dreams to my departed.

You can keep the letter to reread when you feel like it. Others prefer to burn it and feel their words being lifted up to their loved one. There's no right or wrong way to do this kind of ritual. It can create a real closeness and be an extremely personal expression that transcends grief. This ritual can even be so moving that it feels as though you've reached the end of your grief journey.

Are written or spoken affirmations also rituals? Rituals often consist of repeated, intentional words or actions that have personal or symbolic meaning. In that sense, they certainly are. Affirmations can ensure a positive state of mind. They're not usually phrases specifically about the person you've lost, but they create wellness within.

I write affirmations daily to keep myself in the "now" of what I choose to be. I encourage you to make this a daily practice to reset your mindset. You will be able to retain emotional strength and a positive perspective that enables you to approach each morning and retire each night with the knowledge that you are achieving what you have intended to.

Affirmations can also be specific to healing grief, however. Write or say these affirmations every morning or evening (or both). You can create your own, too. These are just suggestions.

- I allow myself to grieve in my own way, in my own time.

- I can seek support from others who love me and understand my grief.

- I honor my loved one's memory by carrying their legacy in my heart.

- I am strong enough to journey through grief and come out even stronger.

- Healing is a process. My healing happens at my own pace.

- My feelings are valid. I can experience them without judgment.

- Even while I am grieving, my memories give me comfort and peace.

- The love of my departed one still lives within me.

- Grief is a journey, not a destination.

- I acknowledge the pain of grief but treat myself with kindness.

I also have a ritual mantra that is like an affirmation. It has been reverberating in my mind for decades: *Today I will be the best possible person I can be.*

You too can gain comfort in your emotional awareness by conducting some mind-work like the exercises I have covered in this chapter. You have traveled a difficult road, but now you can see how emotional growth can be achieved. The sense of sadness does continue, and grief is dark. But it can lighten.

Key Takeaways

- Every human being leaves a legacy. You can gain comfort from discovering your loved one's legacy.

- A beautiful moment of reflection and recollection to think of the legacy of the departed can be very powerful.

- There are many ways you can honor the legacy of your loved one, from physical memorials to personal rituals that you perform. If you don't know how to begin, start by practicing affirmations.

- Rituals of remembrance can also be a very powerful way to remember and commemorate your departed.

- You have traveled a difficult road, but now you can see how emotional growth can be achieved.

Section 3:

The Rest of Your Journey

Chapter 9:

Living Life With Loss

Spring

New life; Rebirth; Continuance

The journey through grief allows for emotional awareness and growth through self-discovery and determining how to live your life through loss. The life skills you've retained through grief have created a tapestry of regeneration. Embrace the new you, warts and all. Love that person looking back at you in the mirror. Live your life to the fullest. Emotional freedom is exhilarating!

Coping With Trauma

Experiencing the trauma of prolonged grief makes the journey to healing extremely difficult, and it takes both time and patience. Complications come not just from the circumstances surrounding the tragic event itself but also from how they affect you as a survivor. However, you've learned that your grief journey is unique to you. No one else will experience the same symptoms in the same order or for the same amount of time.

You now understand the grief dynamic and the various stages of grief that you've gone through. And you've developed healthy coping mechanisms to replace irrational thoughts and negative emotions.

You've learned that consuming negative emotions can change aspects of your brain function and personality. Your suffering from these factors may have gone undetected for a long time. Or the changes in you could have been brushed aside as a normal reaction to the traumatic event. Instead of getting over your grief quickly, you've experienced prolonged or complicated grief. When you suffer from this kind of grief, you can feel the psychological effects for many years. Seeking professional help is a preferred way to address this concern.

You may have projected the negative emotions that have been fueled by tragedy onto benign, uninvolved people. Or you may have attributed those feelings to ordinary stimuli rather than psychological triggers. You now know that there can be stimuli that create a flood of negative emotions that can keep you from having a decent quality of life.

Sadly, you may have suffered in silence. Anxiety and depression hid your symptoms from individuals who could support you. This may happen if you withdraw from society or if your friends and family members retreat from you because they don't know how to help. Other people who notice your negative reactions may think they're just the natural results of experiencing trauma and not an identified and diagnosed psychological disorder.

There Is Hope

Even though you may not see how your pain and grief can be resolved, there are many sources of professional help that you can access. Some, like suicide survivors' groups or crime victims' and families' healing groups, are related to the particular kind of trauma that you've suffered.

Others are less specific, dealing with bereavement in general. You can usually find one through your mental health practitioner, doctor, a hospital, or a recommendation from a friend.

Doctors, psychiatrists, psychologists, trauma counselors, and bereavement group facilitators will be able to help you as well. They can point you toward the interventions and treatments you may need.

In Western societies, we are fortunate to have an array of specialist groups, organizations, professionals, information, and resources to address emotional and behavioral distress brought on by experiencing trauma. People in other countries may not have access to similar support. They may need to do research to find resources that will help them heal from prolonged grief. In Chapter 10, I provide some that you can use to start your search.

Support networks are also crucial to the healing process. Family, loved ones, and friends will feel the need to help and comfort you, even if they don't know precisely what you are going through. Unconditional love and encouragement are vital to your healing, and if you can find them in the people around you, so much the better. It can be difficult for them to ascertain precisely what you are enduring, but they may well understand that this is a serious situation that requires nonjudgmental care and nurturing. If you have this kind of support, you are truly lucky.

These people can continue to support you with love and understanding as you journey out of grief and into hope. You should continue to rely on them without becoming too dependent on them. They can be a help to you even as you transition back into a life that is rich and fulfilling.

It's important to note that each small step you take in your grief journey is tremendously significant. I've seen this occur with clients recovering from trauma. They experience a lightbulb or "aha!" moment when the relief caused by an intervention or a positive thought takes hold. One day, you could begin to have a simple understanding of how you are being controlled by distorted or irrational thoughts, for example. Enthusiasm will take over, and hope will seem ever more possible.

Understanding a specific trigger and how it stirs negative emotions means that you will have a less adverse reaction to a potentially troubling event because you are prepared. Realizing that you are experiencing emotional projection and changing your perception can bring on a desired behavior. Because you have endured so much pain and anguish for a long time, once there is a victory in your recovery—no matter how small—it can give you hope and assurance that you are on the path to recovery. The sheer relief from a successful psychological intervention will be uplifting and inspiring for you.

As you develop new routines, you need to incorporate the healing techniques you've learned into your everyday life. Self-care and mindfulness are not just practices that have helped you deal with grief. They're positive actions and healthy coping mechanisms that you can call on whenever you're experiencing a setback—or even when you're not. Anything that brings you good feelings will help you embrace change and cherish your memories.

Emotional Freedom

Coping with prolonged grief and the trauma associated with it requires a committed effort to regain rationality and control your emotions. Rituals of self-awareness and emotional control need to become a daily practice. Once this occurs and becomes second nature, there will be an emotional freedom that will be exhilarating.

You can easily get annoyed with the overused phrases that the people around you say: The journey is long; the road is bumpy. A grieving person can become frustrated when they hear these sentences. Why? Because they state the bloody obvious! But more than that, the statements do not capture the full extent of what you have endured. You have gained insight. You have guidelines and a roadmap to help you through grief. So, let's do away with the clichés!

The emotional experiences with trauma can be overwhelming. The pain and anguish are inevitable. You do need time to process the associated grief. The difficulty is that you need to be able to feel grief before healing can start. Much of what I've covered in this series enables you to comprehend and develop an understanding of what is occurring in your life. In your own time and factoring in your frame of reference, there are interventions, suggestions, and guidance to address and counteract aspects of trauma experience and its repercussions that you can access.

There are significant times when sudden mind shifts occur. That's a cue for a nervous system that has been starved of positivity. The actual brain structure itself can start recovering. Sudden comprehension can occur. I spoke of mindset through the latter stages of grief, when you reach a certain point and state: "My loved one would not want their legacy to be my continual sadness, misery, and sorrow," or "If I remain in misery and heartache, two lives are missing out on living." These are examples of how understanding occurs when the time is right for the person suffering. Recovery can take an upward spiral from this point.

Emotional awareness develops into emotional growth once you master your human understanding. Use the techniques and strategies you've learned to understand your thought processes and make corrections to distortions or irrationality. Self-talk (your inner voice) will become a companion rather than an annoying foe. It will become a positive component of life instead of a way that your brain punishes you. Realistic goals and expectations will make your journey easier.

That is emotional growth. You become your own best friend. You have developed resilience through perseverance, and you have gained the life skills to make corrections along the way. You've searched for meaning and purpose in your life, and you've found them. You've integrated your memories of the person you've lost with the sense that they are still with you in spirit. You are ready to continue living your life.

You need to develop and retain life skills for your future well-being. Make emotional awareness your constant as you rediscover life, and you'll have reasons to live again. You'll never forget your loved one, friend, or family member, but they would want you to carry on rather than remain in misery. Your memories will come to comfort you instead of tormenting you.

Living With Loss

You never forget your departed friend, loved one, or family member. Sadness does continue, but you have integrated the experience to be able to continue with your life. You have adapted to formulate your identity moving forward. The changes were not necessarily welcomed, but you'll have the confidence to be able to see how you were able to live through loss.

In part, that confidence stems from the emotional awareness and growth that you have experienced. Confidence comes from surviving the trauma of grief and the journey itself. You have optimism now, and that creates opportunity.

You have developed rituals by which you honor and remember your departed. These rituals feel right and sacred, and the closeness and connection they create are comforting. You now have practices of self-improvement that will empower you as you move forward with your life. You've truly learned from the experience of your grief journey.

It was a privilege that you allowed me to walk beside you—that you allowed me to guide you. Helping and counseling you is truly the greatest contribution I can make to your life and the most significant part of my profession. I trust I was able to show you how to find peace.

Key Takeaways

- You do not have to suffer in silence with your prolonged grief. Professional help and assistance are available. Take advantage of it to help with your healing.

- Negative emotions and emotional projection are difficulties you may have encountered. Use the wisdom and experience of your support network to deal with them.

- Even a small step forward in your healing will feel tremendous. When you experience relief because of a new understanding, the revelation of a trigger or other improvements can give you renewed optimism.

- When sudden mind shifts occur, your wounded nervous system will begin to recover.

- Emotional awareness, resilience, and perseverance will make it possible to go on with your life while never forgetting what your loved one has meant to you.

Chapter 10:
Resources by Country

Earth

Home; Existence; Belonging to her; A mantra

You need not walk this path alone! This chapter is a prompt to always research and seek mental and emotional assistance. In it, there are resources to assist you in whichever country you reside. The countries I chose are Amazon's biggest marketplaces. These resources are only the tip of the iceberg. Other nations no doubt also have places to seek first-response assistance.

Finding Help

If you're having thoughts of suicide or self-harm, or you're simply overwhelmed by your emotions and thoughts, you can and should seek help at any time of the day or night.

There are helplines that you can reach by phone or online, and some others that allow you to text them for help. Many of them are toll-free. Trained volunteers or mental health professionals are available to help you with specific problems or just to talk. The hours that each helpline operates may vary, but there are many that can be contacted 24/7. Some will contact the authorities if you are in immediate danger of serious harm, but unless that is the case, they ensure confidentiality.

If your country isn't listed here or you have a more specific need, such as psychological help for veterans, a quick Google search will most likely put you in touch with someone who can help you.

Australia

- **Immediate risk of harm:** 000

- **Suicide callback service:** suicidecallbackservice.org.au; 1300 659 467

- **Lifeline** for anyone having a personal crisis: lifeline.org.au; 13 11 14

- **Beyond Blue** for anxiety and depression: beyondblue.org.au; 1300 22 4636

- **Kids Helpline** for ages 5-25: kidshelpline.com.au; 1800 55 1800

- **MensLine Australia** for men with emotional or relationship concerns: mensline.org.au; 1300 78 99 78

- **Open Arms** for veterans and their families: openarms.gov.au; 1800 011 046

Brazil

- **Centro de Valorização da Vida** suicide and crisis line: 24/7 volunteers; cvv.org.br; 188

- **Central de Atendimento Feminino** for women: 180

- **Sociedade de Amigos Voluntarios SAV-SAMARITANOS:** (081) 3231-4141

Canada

- **Emergency number:** 988

- **Talk Suicide Canada:** 1-833-456-4566 toll-free 24/7; or text 45645 4 p.m. to midnight ET

- **First Nations and Inuit Hope for Wellness Help Line:** 1-855-242-3310

- **Kids Help Phone:** 1-800-668-6868

- **Native Youth Crisis Hotline:** 1-877-209-1266

Denmark

- **BørneTelefonen:** 24/7 volunteers; https://bornetelefonen.dk/; 116 111

- **Mental Health Helpline:** volunteer; psykiatrifonden.dk; 39 25 25 25

- **Livslinien:** 70 201 201

- **Startlinjen** mental health support: 3536 2600; 4 p.m.–11 p.m.

France

- **SOS Amitié:** 24/7 volunteers; 09 72 39 40 50

- **Suicide écoute:** 01 45 39 40 00

- **SOS Help:** 01 46 21 46 46

- **EPE idF Fil Sante Jeunes:** 0800 235 236; chat: https://www.filsantejeunes.com/tchat-individuel

Germany

- **Emotional support helpline:** 116 123

- **TelefonSeelsorge:** 0800 111 0 111; 0800 111 0 222

- **International Helpline Berlin:** 030-44 01 06 07

India

- **AASRA:** 24/7; 91 22 27546669

- **Jeevan Aastha Helpline:** 0091 6576453841

- **SAATH:** 0091 79 26305544

- **SNEHA:** 4424640050

- **SA-MUDRA YUVA Helpline:** 9880396331

- **SAHAI Helpline:** 080–25497777

- **1 Life, Crisis Support, Suicide Prevention:** 78930 78930

- **CHILDLINE 1098:** 1098

- **DISHA-1056:** 1056

- **Mpower 24x7 Mental Health Helpline:** 1800 120 820050

- **ROSHNI:** 040 66202000 or 66202001

Italy

- **Telefono Amico Italia:** 199 284 284

- **Servizio per la Prevenzione del Suicidio—linea di ascolto "Parla con Noi":** 06 33777740

- **Telefono Amico Centri in Rete:** 800 848 400

- **Samaritans— ONLUS:** 06 77208977

Japan

- **Childline Japan:** 0120-99-7777

- **Inochi no Denwa Suicide Hotline:** 03-6634-2556

- **Tell Japan:** 03-5774-0992

- **Anata no Ibasho (Ibashochat.org):** https://talkme.jp/chat

- **Iwate Suicide Prevention Center:** 019-621-9090

- **BW Tokyo Japan:** +81 (0) 3 5286 9090

Mexico

- **SAPTEL:** (55) 5259-8121

- **Línea De La Vida:** 1 800-911-2000

Netherlands

- **Emotional support helpline:** 116123

- **de Luisterlijn:** 0900 0767

- **113 Zelfmoordpreventie:** 0900-0113

- **MIND Korrelatie:** 900 1450

New Zealand

- **1737 Need to Talk:** 1737 (text and call)

- **0508 TAUTOKO:** 0508 828 865

- **Anxiety Helpline:** 0800 269 4389

- **Depression Helpline:** 0800 111 757

- **Shakti Crisis Line:** (women) 0800 742 584

Spain

- **Llama a la vida:** 024

- **Samaritans in Spain:** 900 525 100

- **Teléfono de la Esperanza:** 717 003 717

- **Suicide Hotline:** 914590050

- **Psikevirtual:** 91 290 71 77

- **Suicide Hotline:** 900 925 555

United Kingdom

- **National Suicide Helpline UK:** 0800 689 5652

- **Samaritans UK & Ireland:** 116123

- **Calm:** (men) 0800 585858

- **HopeLine UK:** 0800 068 4141; text: 07860039967

- **Lifeline** (Northern Ireland)**:** 0808 808 8000

- **Premier Lifeline:** (Christian) 0300 111 0101

- **Breathing Space:** (Scotland) 0800 83 85 87

- **Anxiety UK:** 03444 775 774

- **Mind:** 0300 123 3393; (Birmingham) 0121 262 3555

- **No Panic:** 0844 967 4848

- **OCD Action:** 0300 636 5478; 44 20 7253 5272

- **SANE:** 0300 304 7000

- **Childline:** 0800 1111

- **Cruse Bereavement Care:** 0808 808 1677

- **Beat** (eating disorders): 0808 801 0677 (adult); 0808 801 0711 (under 18)

- **Rural Support:** 0800 138 1678

- **Self-Injury Support:** 0808 800 8088

- **YoungMinds—Parents Helpline:** 0808 802 5544

- **Maytree:** 020 7263 7070

- **Hope Project:** (men) 0117 909 6630

United States

- **Didi Hirsch Suicide Prevention Center:** (800) 273 8255

- **IMALIVE:** 2025363200

- **National Suicide Prevention Lifeline:** 988 or 800-273-8255 or 1-888-628-9454 or 1-800-799-4889

- **Veteran/Military Crisis Line:** 1 800 273 8255

- **Crisis Text Line:** Text HOME to 741741

- **National Alliance on Mental Illness HelpLine:** 1-800-950-(6264)

Conclusion

Sunrise

Glory; Renewal; Hopefulness

Everyone experiences grief in very different and personal ways. You can't compare the depth of your grief, the amount of time you've been feeling it, or the symptoms of it with anyone else affected by trauma. Even people in the same family experiencing the same trauma, such as when a beloved relative is diagnosed with a terminal illness, will not necessarily experience it the same way that you do.

I hope this book has allowed people to feel acknowledged and understood for the traumatic situations they are in and the gravity of what has been occurring.

I wrote this book for people trying to deal with grief from a tragic life event. The grief people experience with traumatic occurrences can have compounding mental and emotional aspects that make it very difficult to navigate through. Many other traumatic life events besides the ones covered in this book still involve an intense grieving process. The same principles you've learned here will apply to those situations as well.

In all of the situations covered, it's important to know that you will need a support system, which may include your family doctor, a therapist, your friends and loved ones, and a variety of rehab or hospice personnel.

At the beginning of this book, I discussed prolonged grief disorder and how it differs from "normal" grief. Prolonged grief lasts longer and is more devastating. It can lead to physical and mental damage, which can cause you to be distraught and even disabled, unable to cope with the tasks of daily life. Treatment such as CBT can lessen your grief, however.

The second chapter covered the devastating trauma caused when you lose a friend or loved one to suicide. Your grief is likely to be complicated by all the questions you have about why they did it and whether there was anything you could have done to stop it.

Your brain reacts to grief in predictable ways. Different regions of the brain undergo changes that affect your emotions and thoughts. Powerful brain chemicals become unbalanced, and hormones affect your body as well, leaving you vulnerable to adverse physical conditions as well as the irrational thinking you already have. This brain activity occurs with any kind of trauma and prolonged grief, so it can apply to any of the assorted traumas discussed in each of the chapters. Irrational thoughts result but don't seem irrational at all to the person experiencing the grief.

Although it's not possible to compare traumas and grief exactly, one of the most traumatic life events happens when a friend or loved one dies at the hands of another, whether that be a murder, a drunk driving accident, or a war. When a person has been kidnapped or is missing in action, another layer of trauma and grief is added. Anger and hatred toward the person responsible can be projected onto other, innocent persons around you. As you try to deal with grief over a long period of time, you could even develop PTSD in addition to anxiety and depression. You may experience personality changes that your friends and loved ones will notice.

Strong emotions affect you if you are faced with a loss that occurs early in life—a miscarriage, SIDS death, stillborn child, or death of a child due to an accident or disease. This is one of the most devastating losses that anyone can imagine. Your emotions will be extreme, and it will take a long time for you to process your emotions and thoughts to recover from the traumatic grief. You may feel emotions such as bitterness and blame, as well as a desire for revenge. There may be self-blame involved, too. Triggers you encounter may cause you to relive the traumatic event. Consultation with doctors and therapists will be essential, especially if you develop PTSD because of your traumatic loss.

Other causes of prolonged grief occur if you lose a limb or the function of a limb or limbs caused by a spinal cord injury or an accident. A terminal diagnosis is another situation in which prolonged grief is likely to affect you. Both require a huge change in your circumstances and your mindset. Initial reactions can fluctuate widely, and the reactions and attitudes of those around you can make your journey more difficult.

Trauma can change you! It can change your brain, as noted, but it can also change your personality. Psychologists define emotions, thoughts, and feelings in different ways. Emotions, the first instinctual reaction you have to trauma, lead to thoughts and then to feelings. This process can be disrupted by trauma. You can develop irrational thinking and unhealthy coping mechanisms. Unless you recognize the warning signs and get help for your difficulties, your changed behavior will persist. Once you do recognize the red flags, you are ready to take the next steps toward healing from your prolonged grief.

Triggers—stimuli that relate to the cause of your trauma—can cause you to have intense reactions in which you relive the trauma or have flashbacks. The best way to counter the effects that triggers invoke is emotional awareness. Fortunately, you have a whole team who is there to help you with the process. Your therapist is a very important part of that team. They can use one or more of many techniques to help you understand your condition and make changes that will help. You may find the process painful at first, but if you stick with it, you may find the missing pieces of your mental health and happiness.

Another practice that you can use to relieve your grief is to consider the legacy of the person you have lost. There are many ways to do this. You can donate money to a relevant charity or organization, designate a memorial space, or have a ceremony of remembrance. You can also reflect on other kinds of legacy, such as the wisdom and learning that your loved one has passed on to others. Yet another way to remember their legacy is to develop your own private ritual that you can use to celebrate their memory. Above all, remember that your friend or loved one would not want their legacy to be one of despair and misery. They would want you to live with fond memories, without trauma.

Even though it's difficult to cope with traumatic grief, keep in mind that there is hope. Remember that you have a support group of professionals, friends, and family members who can help you through the difficult times. And remember the techniques they have taught you such as mindfulness and affirmations. Make them a part of your life so that your journey toward healing will continue.

It is life-changing when positive progress occurs. Through repeated life work, thought processing, and self-analysis, you can retrain your brain. When you have honest comprehension and rational thoughts, you can achieve more positive behavior. It can be exhilarating when you realize that disturbing emotions no longer control your life. You now have a process that will continue to aid you whenever grief enters your life again. Essentially, you will become your own therapist.

My nonclinical approach has been the foundation for a positive change in many people over the past two decades. As I've said, for me, professional counseling is a privilege. Someone desperately in need invites me into their life, needing me to address serious issues, simply because they cannot. Thank you for your invitation. There is no greater privilege!

Grief is dark, but it can lighten. Now, there is hope for you to live life fully again.

Book Review

Dear Reader, it has been my privilege to walk with you and guide you at this difficult time.

I trust I was able to show how there can be peace in your life again.

If you found solace in my book, I will be forever grateful if you could leave me a Review.

A moment of your time can encourage more people to benefit from this content.

The QR codes below will direct you to the Review Page or Home Page of this book in your country/marketplace. You can find "Customer Reviews" or "Review this product" on the left-hand side of the Book's Homepage. Your feedback is greatly appreciated.

Thank you.

USA

Australia

UK

https://bit.ly/3T2CfZV

Canada

https://bit.ly/3SLpDVH

References

Appelbaum, P., & Yousif, L. (2022). *Prolonged grief disorder*. American Psychiatric Association. https://www.psychiatry.org/patients-families/prolonged-grief-disorder

Baatz, C. (2018, March 5). *How trauma changes the brain*. The Independence Center. https://www.theindependencecenter.org/how-trauma-changes-the-brain/

Boelen, P. A., Lenferink, L. I. M., & Spuij, M. (2021). CBT for prolonged grief in children and adolescents: A randomized clinical trial. *American Journal of Psychiatry, 178*(4), 294–304. https://doi.org/10.1176/appi.ajp.2020.20050548

CBC Radio. (2018, April 20). *If you want to talk to someone, here's a list of resources that might help*. CBC. https://www.cbc.ca/radio/opp/if-you-want-to-talk-to-someone-here-s-a-list-of-resources-that-might-help-1.4603730

Christopher Reeve: The life of the Man of Steel. (2018, October 5). Aruma. https://www.aruma.com.au/about-us/blog/christopher-reeve-the-life-of-the-man-of-steel/

Dylan Alcott. (n.d.). Olympics. https://olympics.com/en/athletes/dylan-alcott

Dylan Alcott. (n.d.). Sport Australia Hall of Fame. https://sahof.org.au/award-winner/dylan-alcott/

Free telephone counseling hotlines in Canada. (n.d.). OpenCounseling. https://blog.opencounseling.com/hotlines-ca/

Free telephone counseling hotlines in Germany. (n.d.). OpenCounseling. https://blog.opencounseling.com/hotlines-de/

Free telephone counseling hotlines in Spain. (n.d.). OpenCounseling. https://blog.opencounseling.com/hotlines-es/

Free telephone counseling hotlines in the Netherlands. (n.d.). OpenCounseling. https://blog.opencounseling.com/hotlines-nl/

Free telephone counseling hotlines in the Republic of Italy. (n.d.). OpenCounseling. https://blog.opencounseling.com/hotlines-it/

Helpline for depression, suicide and emotional distress. (n.d.). Indianhelpline.com. https://indianhelpline.com/suicide-helpline

Helplines & support. (n.d.). Mental Health Foundation. https://mentalhealth.org.nz/helplines

Helplines, hotlines, and crisis lines from around the world. (n.d.). TherapyRoute. https://www.therapyroute.com/article/helplines-suicide-hotlines-and-crisis-lines-from-around-the-world

International suicide prevention helplines. (2023, January 19). *The New York Times.* https://www.nytimes.com/article/suicide-prevention-helplines.html

Japan suicide hotlines (n.d.). Suicide.org. http://www.suicide.org/hotlines/international/japan-suicide-hotlines.html

Mayo Clinic Staff. (2017). *Complicated grief—Diagnosis and treatment.* Mayo Clinic. https://www.mayoclinic.org/diseases-conditions/complicated-grief/diagnosis-treatment/drc-20360389

Mayo Clinic Staff. (2022, December 13). *Complicated grief—Symptoms and causes*. Mayo Clinic. https://www.mayoclinic.org/diseases-conditions/complicated-grief/symptoms-causes/syc-20360374

Norwood, A. (2017). *Wilma Rudolph*. National Women's History Museum. https://www.womenshistory.org/education-resources/biographies/wilma-rudolph

Suicide hotlines and crisis lines in France. (2020, February 18). TherapyRoute. https://www.therapyroute.com/article/suicide-hotlines-and-crisis-lines-in-france

Sutton, J. (2022, April 1). *How to treat complicated grief in therapy: 12 examples*. Positive Psychology. https://positivepsychology.com/complicated-grief/

Image References

Auzza38. (n.d.). *Hands* [Image]. Pixabay. https://pixabay.com/photos/hand-holding-hands-wedding-pledge-1222229/

Congerdesign. (n.d.). *Cherry blossoms* [Image]. Pixabay. https://pixabay.com/photos/cherry-blossoms-japanese-cherry-3327498/

Jonpauling. (n.d.). *Waterfall* [Image]. Pixabay. https://pixabay.com/photos/waterfall-nature-river-scenery-6619377/

Montanya, J. (n.d.). *Kitten* [Image]. From the author's collection.

MarcusVu. (n.d.). *Dawn* [Image]. Pixabay. https://pixabay.com/photos/dawn-morning-sun-light-sunrise-3008369/

Nutraveller. (n.d.). *Beach* [Image]. Pixabay. https://pixabay.com/photos/beach-ocean-shore-sea-coast-waves-2413081/

Oyso. (n.d.). *Forest* [Image]. Pixabay. https://pixabay.com/photos/forest-trees-fir-trees-woods-6874717/

Pattyjansen. (n.d.). *Ferns* [Image]. Pixabay. https://pixabay.com/photos/ferns-tree-ferns-australia-sydney-303016/

Robert_C. (n.d.). *Trees* [Image]. Pixabay. https://pixabay.com/photos/trees-forest-snow-snowy-cold-4727156/

Scartmyart. (n.d.). *Night* [Image]. Pixabay. https://pixabay.com/photos/night-sky-moon-dark-nature-stars-2938792/

Sharonjoy17. (n.d.). *Rainbow* [Image]. Pixabay. https://pixabay.com/photos/rainbow-river-nature-landscape-2424647/

TomMarc. (n.d.). *Sunset* [Image]. Pixabay. https://pixabay.com/photos/lake-reeds-sunset-landscape-nature-696098/

Wikilmages. (n.d.). *Earth* [Image]. Pixabay. https://pixabay.com/photos/earth-planet-space-world-universe-11009/